VITAL SIGNS 1

Bringing Together Reading and Writing

Edited by
James L. Collins
University at Buffalo

Boynton/Cook Publishers
Heinemann
Portsmouth, NH

Boynton/Cook Publishers
A Division of
Heinemann Educational Books, Inc.
70 Court Street, Portsmouth, NH 03801
Offices and agents throughout the world

"Blackberrying" from *Crossing the Water*, by Sylvia Plath. Copyright © 1962,
1971 by Ted Hughes. Reprinted by permission of Harper & Row, Publishers, Inc.

ISBN 0-86709-253-X
ISSN 1045-2672

Printed in the United States of America
94 93 92 91 90 9 8 7 6 5 4 3 2 1

Contents

Introduction

Dear Peter:

Just a quick note to share some jottings I made while we talked about our new project.

We want an annual publication addressed to teachers in junior high school through the first year of college: what successful teachers do; good teachers who have misgivings about what they're required to do; reports of lessons, activities, teaching approaches, and student experiences.

We'll use an open-ended approach—organize around a theme after we see what we get. We suggested reader response as one possible focus.

We want to stay away from a "quick fix" approach.

*   *   *

Dear Jim:

Bob and I have talked about what to do regarding our initial persuasions about keeping the project thematically open-ended, at least initially. It sounds sensible but faintly worrisome too; that is, we could readily end up with a nonbook on our hands—a stack of sentiments, policies, and practices too dissonant to provide any overall coherence. (The last thing we want, though, is too blooming much coherence.) So perhaps we'd better come up with something, however amorphous. The three of us, you've noted, did arrive at reader response as one possible topic/theme. (Fifteen or so years in the classroom and I still don't know the difference between the two.)

As for the mix of contributors, we figure about half of them would be working teachers, preferably grades 8–13. Bob will check with Susan Ohanian, a friend and sparkling good writer on matters educational, about whether she has any current language-related issue she wants to bloody.

As for editorial boards, the hell with them. It's as simple as keeping the contents topical and current and avoiding hackneyed contentions. No need to drag in a pack of second-guessers. And as for editorial policy itself, we are, as you know, somewhere between cutting-edge and fuzzy-headed liberal.

*   *   *

Dear Peter:

I don't think we need a theme for the first volume as much as we need an organizing idea for the whole project. I'd like a title to make it easier to contemplate and discuss what we're doing, to give purpose and focus to the idea of a Heinemann–Boynton/Cook annual volume.

*   *   *

Dear Jim:

How about *Vital Signs*?

*   *   *

Dear Peter:

Yes! *Vital Signs* would make a good title. "Vital signs" in the sense of important and necessary ideas—ideas reflecting life, energy, power in language teaching. Our focus will be on what's right with the teaching of English.

*   *   *

Dear Peter:

Arthur Applebee, Bruce Miller, and Gill Clarkson have agreed to do pieces for *Vital Signs*, and about half a dozen others so far have said they'll try to send something. I wrote to Susan Ohanian, but I haven't heard from her yet. Charlie Moran is planning a very promising piece on having students write creatively, in the manner of the author they're about to study, before they read the work.

I'd like to include somewhere short pieces such as the one Charlie did on Cliff's Notes. This will help make the volume more than only a collection of papers. I want to give the book, partly at least, the character of a dialogue with teachers, and the Cliff's Notes paragraph has that quality because it speaks clearly and invites thought and comment.

*　　*　　*

Dear Susan:

The project is further along than when I last wrote, and I can give you some idea of the book's contents. Perhaps you'll notice a niche you'd like to fill with a contribution.

The book is about the teaching and learning of literature. As I believe I mentioned to you, I'm thinking of "Literature as a Performing Art" as a subtitle. The papers I've selected so far adhere more or less directly to the principles that readers are performers and that too often the teacher's reading is the only performance allowed in the classroom. So, the book presents an alternative to the teaching of literature as received interpretation, in which the teacher leads the class through lecture and discussion to the teacher's interpretation. That idea is from Arthur Applebee's contribution.

The book is organizing itself into two parts. The first part contains several papers on our motives for reading and teaching literature. One main point, but far from the only one in this section, is that literature study might be the only place in school where kids can learn to think and enjoy for themselves—at least the only legal place. There's room here for an irreverent piece on the uses of literature for purposes of socialization, such as the "literature as vehicle of cultural literacy" position.

The second part of the book is the more practical section. It contains pieces describing how teachers go about giving kids more than the usual limited degree of freedom in responding to literature. Most of the pieces are written for teachers; a couple, however, could be read with pleasure by students. I'm looking for alternatives to what my daughter described, during her first encounter with Shakespeare, this way: "First they have us read the play. Then they have us read it out loud. Then they read parts to us, telling us what they mean. Then they have us write about what we've said about the play. Don't they trust us?"

*   *   *

Dear Louise,

I enjoyed listening to and talking with you at dinner on Sunday night, and I want you to know you've helped me think about the project I'm working on.

When I began to think about "Literature as a Performing Art" as a subtitle, I had in mind not only the papers in *Vital Signs*, but also a remembrance of my own teaching. Twenty years ago, in my first year as a high school English teacher, I taught *The Old Man and the Sea* to tenth-graders. I was just out of graduate school, an MAT in teaching English, and I was determined to do my best teaching, indeed the best teaching anyone could do. I commented at least once on every page, and I must have poked and prodded every idea and event in the novel for its import. Of course I included plot, character, setting, symbol, conflict, theme, and all the rest. Just when I was pointing to a similarity between Santiago and Jesus Christ, I was interrupted by Kenny, a student memorable after all these years for his ambition to dance professionally. Kenny said this to me: "You don't read the way we do." A performer himself, he was measuring my performance and asking for a chance to do his own.

So I hope *Vital Signs* will persuade and equip more teachers to give students the chance to perform literary works for themselves. Of course, a reluctance to let students do more of the work of making texts meaningful might stem from the fact that teachers, after all, are good at interpreting texts. They are highly trained, are well rehearsed, and get paid to perform for an audience of 30 or so spectators at once. Can students be trusted to discover the same full meanings as teachers? A remark you made after dinner helps answer that question affirmatively. When I told you that I've been thinking of "Literature as a

Performing Art" as a subtitle, you said that you had appended an essay called "Coda: A Performing Art" to the second edition of *Literature as Exploration*. Not wanting you to think I had borrowed your title, I quickly responded with, "I thought I had invented that!" You replied with, "That's OK. More than one person can invent the same idea." That observation, that more than one person can invent an idea, leads us out of the fear that students won't get sufficiently responsible meanings from texts unless we provide the meanings fully achieved and neatly packaged. Students can invent ideas during their reading of literature, and it's important that we give them opportunities to do so, since it's the inventing that matters most.

What, then, is left for teachers to do? Should they just keep their fingers out of the wheels and let students read freely? Obviously not, because leaving students to their own devices might often be asking them to struggle with challenges beyond their capacities. The real work of teaching literature is in providing experiences that develop reading and responding abilities for individuals, for partners and groups in collaboration, and for whole classes. Describing such experiences is what the essays in *Vital Signs* are about.

* * *

Dear Peter,

Another update on *Vital Signs*.

Some statistics on the project: I've accepted 15 pieces so far, and I hope to get one more, Susan Ohanian's. Six of the accepted 15 are authored by high school teachers; 12 of the 15 describe practical teaching and learning strategies; 4 papers explore reasons for reading and teaching literature; one piece, Susan Beth Pfeffer's on family matters, is in a class by itself (though, as I'll mention in a minute, it connects with the others).

The book has two main parts, Motives and Methods. The Motives section explores reasons for reading literature and for helping students become engaged with literature. The Methods section presents practical ideas and strategies for teaching and learning literature, and two main categories in the Methods section are Responding and Storytelling. Throughout all this, the emphasis is on literature in the active lane.

The piece by Susan Beth Pfeffer is called "Family Matters" and could fit in either part of the book. It could belong under Motives because it has something lighthearted to say about why she writes—for revenge on family members. And it could belong under Methods in the Storytelling section because it tells stories and reminds readers to have some fun with literature, just as authors sometimes do. Like the book, Pfeffer's piece questions the overly serious, even doleful attitude usually hovering in the background of literature study. "Family Matters" tells us gently to lighten up a bit. I'm sure teachers will enjoy Pfeffer's essay and will even want to share it with students.

I'm thinking of putting Bruce Miller's piece first in the Motives section, and Pfeffer's last in the Methods section. The two papers, neither one of which is directly about teaching literature, will then frame the volume. Miller's title is "Why Do We Read Literature?" and the "We" refers to devoted readers, those who consume literature with passion. Certainly we would like to think we are creating such readers in our classrooms, but we obviously don't have a nation of lovers of literature. Could be it's time to ask why devoted readers read, and then let the answers influence what we do in classrooms.

*   *   *

Dear Peter:

I talked with Marni Schwartz last night, and she said that Susan Ohanian is, indeed, writing something for us.

Marni's own piece is excellent. It's on storytelling as a means of engaging with literature. Certainly the reading of a story must be enhanced by preparing it for telling, and the experience of a story must be deepened by telling it to someone else.

Marni's final draft arrived just as I was thinking about changing the subtitle from "Literature as a Performing Art" to something else. Her piece encourages me to make the change. She and her students don't perform stories, at least not in the sense of actors performing for audiences. She tells stories by stepping inside them and inviting others in. This is consistent with what we've meant by literature as a performing art: performing literary works by reading in ways that entail understanding of the work. Storytelling is one example of reading to enhance understanding of literature, and the book is filled with others. Trouble is, when I mention "Literature as a Performing Art," people think I'm talking about creative dramatics or something similar. I'll continue thinking about changing the subtitle and get back to you. By the way, Joan Mittelstaedt's piece is also about storytelling, in her case as a means of engaging nonacademic kids with mythology. She believes her students deserve the same opportunities as college-bound kids.

* * *

Dear Peter:

Susan Ohanian's piece has arrived and it's *great*. I placed it at the front of the collection because it sets the tone for the rest.

Susan mentions students who fake reading, and that prompted me to go ahead and change our subtitle. I'll explain the change by telling a story.

It's the last day of school in June, and I'm exchanging pleasantries and banter with members of my third-period class. They're seniors and, of course, their mood is highly elevated as we wait for the bell signaling the end of our year's work together. We talk a little about college plans and also about jobs, since most of them won't be going to college, at least not right away. Finally the bell rings, and we say things like, "Goodbye and have a good summer." as they file out for the last time. Kathy, always an excellent student, says how much she enjoyed the course and others immediately agree. I also endure a couple of parting shots. Eddie reminds me that when I passed out copies of *Hamlet*, he collected them right behind me. And Richard has something even more unforgettable to say. He stops in front of me, smiles delightedly, and reports in a voice that lets me know he thinks he's beaten the system: "You know, Mr. Collins, I never read any of those books."

The story is true. What's more, Richard had, indeed, beaten the system. I had worked so hard at teaching literature that my students didn't have to do much work at all—they didn't even have to read the books. "Literature as a Performing Art," our old subtitle, could mean, ironically, pretending you're doing the reading.

Come to class and listen, and you've done enough to pass. Literature study through an intermediary, the teacher. The teacher as translator. Or, to switch to an electronic metaphor, the teacher as literature processor.

The first issue of *Vital Signs* takes a different pedagogical stance. The book is mostly about enhancing the experience of literature. Not only by listening to the teacher or by doing things after the reading of literature, such as discussing and answering questions. It's about enhancing the actual reading of literature, sustaining the moment where reader and text come together. Helping students with the process of experiencing literature means supporting their persistent and hard grappling with the subject at hand, their reading. No pain, no gain. And it also means helping them to enjoy the process. No pleasure, no gain.

Part One
MOTIVES

Literature is experience. Readers can substitute another's experience with a poem for their own reading no more effectively than they can substitute another's hearing of a musical work for their own.

—*Robert Probst*

Literature Has No Uses

Susan Ohanian

*I*n a column titled "Internal Combustion Prose," Russell Baker noted the defeat of a proposal to emblazon Wisconsin license plates with the slogan "Eat Cheese or Die." Maybe the born-again Whole Languagelicals who have recently discovered books should take up from where the folks in Wisconsin left off. Certainly schoolmarm slogans, which run along the lines of "I love reading," could use a bit more oomph. The battle-cry rhetoric of "Read or Die" has the kind of zip to wake people up. Some professional organization might even want to stick it on their next batch of T-shirts, coffee mugs, and bumper-stickers.

Reading, as everyone knows, deserves all the help it can get. Some folk think schools are filled with reading. They are wrong. Reading disappears about midway through the third grade. After that, students spend their time writing term papers and getting ready for the SATs. They copy passages out of encyclopedias and answer questions on ditto sheets titled *How Well Did You Read?* The gifted get enrichment courses in footnoting. And it doesn't take any of these kids a day and a half to figure out that when you gotta write a term paper and answer the questions at the end of the chapter, reading only slows you down.

I once taught in an alternative high school where I was responsible for 40 disaffected students who can best be labeled as "None of the above." Our classroom was filled with daily copies of the local paper, the *New York Times*, and the *Daily News*, and paperbacks of every type—best sellers, thrillers, mysteries, romances, joke books, science fiction, sports, biographies, essays, how-to books. Every few weeks I took a few students to the local bookstore to help choose more books.

We had a lot of single copies of traditional English classroom books on the shelves. Students seemed to get reassurance from seeing *A Tale of Two Cities, Julius Caesar,* and so forth. They had no intention of reading such books, but they liked knowing the books were there. A student would pick up *A Tale of Two Cities*, exclaim, "Oh, yeah," and put it down. These books made the place look like a real school. In this, my students' attitude toward the classics was akin to the position espoused by E.D. Hirsch—actually reading the classics is not necessary, but name recognition provides some comfort.

All of my students *could* read; they just didn't. I insisted that the first rule of our classroom was that every student read half an hour a day. They were all expert at faking reading. How I got them reading is a rather involved story, but it wasn't by ordering 40 copies of *The Old Man and the Sea*. Once a student got hooked on a book—be it *Flowers for Algernon*, *The Outsiders*, *Temple of Gold*, *Richie*, or something else—other students noticed and demanded, "Let me see."

I kept tabs on things but didn't interrogate those students about their understanding of plot, theme, rising action, and so forth. I judged a book a success when a student closed the last page and asked, "Do you have any more?" On their own, about three-fourths of the students began stretching the obligatory half-hour period into an hour a day. And more. Even those who stuck to the half-hour reading were amazed. They told me they'd read more books in the three months in my classroom than they had read in 11 years in regular school. In traditional classrooms, kids are too busy answering questions to do much reading.

I know some colleagues will agree with the inspector from the State Education Department: All this reading may be fine in its place, but it isn't Literature. He saw students reading Dick Francis, Paul Zindel, Adam Hall, William Goldman, Paula Danzinger, and Cynthia Voigt and complained about the quality of our Literature. I pointed out that many of the students had also read John Updike, Frank Conroy, *Unicorn in the Garden*, *Incident at Owl Creek*, Poe stories, excerpts from Anne Frank's *Diary*, *Hiroshima*. After watching the movie *Night and Fog*, we examined the rhetoric of Hoess' testimony at Nuremburg and accounts of responsibility at Mai-Lai. One student and I had a very impassioned discussion following his reading of Bettelheim's *Truants from Life*. And so on. But the inspector complained of our lack of class sets of "the standard books." He asked, "What major work do your sophomores read?" I replied that I didn't think we had any sophomores at the moment. And then I wrote a letter of protest to the State Education Department, insisting that if they wished to send out any more inspectors they should do it after school hours, as I would not again subject my students to anybody sneering at the books that overflowed our shelves and stimulated our minds.

State Education bureaucrats, of course, are not the only folk who worry about real Literature. Very early in my career I taught at a technological university. My freshman engineering students, able readers all, hated English class as much as any reluctant reader I have ever encountered. It became my mission to find wonderful words—to demonstrate the power of language—to them. Every day I wrote snippets on the board for their wonder, amazement, laughter. And every day I worried and fretted over what novel we would read in the spring. And then *Harper's* ran an excerpt of Norman Mailer's *On the Steps of the Pentagon*, announcing the book would be published simultaneously in hardback and paperback.

I read that magazine excerpt and knew that I had found our book. My professorial colleagues stewed and fretted and muttered, "Well, yes, it is powerful, but it is Literature?" My students and I read that book—we laughed, argued, fumed, worried, and reached no consensus. We were moved, angered, challenged, and, I think, changed by that book.

I told my students about the faculty concern that the book might not be Literature but that if it wasn't then I had no idea what Literature was. And then, weeks after we'd finished the book and moved on to others, *On the Steps of the Pentagon* won the Pulitzer Prize for Literature and the National Book Award. My students, the fellows who hated English, came dashing into the room to congratulate me. I think they must have been nearly as pleased as Norman Mailer. I never taught the book again. It was a book that was perfect for those particular students at that particular moment. And the next term, the book, certified Literature, was on the reading list in half a dozen Literature courses at the university.

Am I contradicting myself? First I say "Don't make 25 third- or eighth- or tenth-graders all read the same book," and then I tell of making 100 college freshmen all read the same book. College freshmen have tougher constitutions and they are a whole lot easier to teach, mold, coerce, and dominate than eighth-graders. College freshmen have similar purposes and goals. But whom are we talking about when we talk about an eighth-grader? The girl who spells her name "Sherri" and hides a copy of *True Confessions* in her binder? Or the "Sherry" who sucks her thumb and wants to listen to a tape of "Rumpelstiltskin"? Sherri/Sherry can't be pinned down to read the same book on different days of the week, let alone the same book as all of her classmates.

This sort of problem did not seem to trouble William Bennett when he compiled the list of recommended books for seventh- and eighth-graders in his James Madison Elementary School. And I don't hear an outcry against Bennett's list from teachers or professional organizations. As a profession we find it easier to run for cover than to stand and fight. When governors and industrialists announced their concern for excellence in the schools, for example, instead of pointing out that these emperors of excellence were naked, my professional organization issued an excellence sweatshirt. I worry that at this very moment they might be appointing a joint subcommittee to figure out ways to turn such Bennett favorites as *The Scarlet Pimpernel*, *The Yearling*, *Ivanhoe*, and *The Virginian* into memo pads. Or a bumper sticker.

As for me, I want my T-shirt to read "Literature has no uses." Certainly it is foolish to call on Literature to redress the trade deficit, increase the gross national product, and help kids say "No." Worse than foolish, it is wrong.

William Bennett thinks that seventh- and eighth-graders should read the recommended books closely "for theme, style, point of view, plot, setting, character, mood, irony, and imagery." And that's not all! Like those ads on TV for the $14.95 kitchen knife that also waxes, polishes, and whistles "Dixie," Bennett promises that these books will also "serve as models of fine composition and as subjects for writing assignments that stress a mastery of elementary vocabulary, grammar, usage, mechanics, description, persuasion, narration, and exposition."

Before we try to decide what the kids should read and how they should read it, maybe we'd do well to think about why we want them to read. What is this thing called Literature, and why do we want kids to do it? That is a serious question, one every teacher should face. And I'm not talking about such tripe as *pre-reading*, *setting purposes*, and *getting the lesson objective on the board*. One of our professional journals printed an unwittingly hilarious article that should be the final word on pre-reading piffle. The punchline to the good professor's advice was that if the children were going to read about ducks, then the teacher could set the purpose by waddling into the room like a duck. Twenty years in classrooms from grades 1 through 14 have proven to me that when we bring the best words possible to particular students at a particular ready moment in their lives, that is a great big lolloping enough. There's no need to quack, waddle, or pop.

But looking neither to the right nor the left, many teachers will feel compelled to jump to add a classic or two to their curriculum. Too many of us would rather jump than be shoved. And these days we worry as much about the media as the principal and the board of education. Any day now I expect to find a Gallup Pollster on my doorstep, taking a body count to find out how many of my students have read *The Virginian*. And then *USA Today* can print a front-page colored graph on the state of classics in the classroom as related to gross national product. The *New York Times* will run the same graph in black and white on page 46.

And nobody will ask, "Did anybody enjoy the book?" Does any thirteen-year-old ask, on finishing *Ivanhoe*, *The Red Pony*, or *Rip Van Winkle*, "Are there more?"

People get nervous when I poke fun at Sir Walter Scott. But I would advise any defenders to pick up *Ivanhoe* and read it before sending me their angry letters. Nobody reads *Ivanhoe* these days, but nobody wants to be quoted as denouncing it either. I asked teachers, librarians, and professors from all over the country about Mr. Bennett's list and the even-more-ridiculous *Summertime Favorites* list put forth by the National Endowment for the Humanities. (Would you believe *The Pilgrim's Progress* as a summertime favorite for seventh- and eighth-graders?) The general reaction was one of relief: "Yes we do this one and this one. . . ." *Doing* a book, of course, means watching a movie, making puppets, listening to the teacher read aloud, answering questions, looking up vocabulary. *Doing* is far different from reading.

I suppose that one time or another in my career my students and I have talked about the theme in one book, the style of another, and maybe even the setting in another. Never all at once. Most often, I keep my mouth shut when a student finishes a book. I certainly don't ask how many ducks were on the pond. Such interfering school talk makes one reluctant to pick up another book. When I phoned a friend long distance recently and told her, "You must read Tobias Wolff's *This Boy's Life* (The Atlantic Monthly Press, 1989)—and while you're at it read Geoffrey Wolff's *The Duke of Deception* written 10 years ago," I talked about the Wolffs' incredible memoirs of childhood for half an hour without ever mentioning setting, plot, theme, or whatever. That's just not the way real people read real books. Not when they are really excited by them, anyway.

For me, reading, like writing, is a private act. I regard committees as the last refuge of the scoundrel, and *collaboration* is just a fancy word for committee. Certainly there are times when beginning readers help each other learn to read; there are times when passages scream to be read aloud to a friend. But ask yourself: "When was the last time you and 24 other people sat down and read the same book together?" I can't even get my husband to read the same books I do.

And I sure don't know 24 other people who want to read the books I want to read. When I want to read them. Once I actually tried to get about 20 people all involved in the same story. When Max Apple's "Stranger at the Table" appeared in *Esquire*, I was so moved by the story I photocopied it and sent it to everybody I knew. I mean that quite literally. I was working in California at the time and all my ex-colleagues in New York began getting thick envelopes with the imperative "READ THIS!" scrawled on the 10-page story inside. I was surprised when I didn't get ecstatic phone calls or letters back. I thought at least half a dozen people would report that the story inspired a moment of epiphany. But then I made a few calls and I could sense people were as puzzled as hell. I'm not Jewish, they weren't Jewish, so how come I was sending them this story about keeping kosher? A few people said, "Uh, it was interesting." I got so wound up in the whole thing that I ended up writing Max Apple to clarify an argument I had with my boss over that story and another one he wrote. I'm not sure Apple's reply was at all clarifying, but it sure was fun.

The only other time I wrote to an author was when I was a college freshman and I asked E. M. Forster a straightforward question about "The Celestial Omnibus." He sent me a straightforward answer, and I was startled by my professor's astonishment when I showed him Forster's reply. "Why would you do that?" he demanded. Ever since, I have wondered if maybe that's why teachers like teaching dead authors: smart-aleck kids can't write letters behind their backs. And all this makes me think I'd like to write Tobias Wolff. I really want to know if that sneaking, lying, irrepressible boy is okay. I care a lot about that boy. I feel certain any teacher would.

In *The Call of Stories* (Houghton Mifflin, 1989), Robert Coles quotes William Carlos Williams' worry that teachers elicit dependence rather than independence in their students: "When you graduate from college and read a book, whose office hours do you visit when you have a question?" Do we convince our students that they need either a teacher or Cliff's Notes to read a book? Will they ever be tempted to pick up a book without one of us peering over their shoulders? Do we ever convince them that reading can be a whole lot of fun?

We must beware of what Walker Percy calls the "busy disregard" of the tourist. He is so preoccupied with his camera or how much to tip or whether to drink the water—the mechanics of the matter—that he misses the foreign locale entirely. Literature teachers are in danger of that same "busy disregard"—getting caught up in the mechanics of Literature and missing the point of why anybody would want to read.

Back in the '70s I polled 600 seventh-, eighth-, and ninth-graders, asking them a number of questions about what Language Arts is and why they are required to study it. The student response to "How can language arts help you when you get out of school?" was depressingly utilitarian. The majority of students felt that Language Arts was the ticket to getting a job—in the narrowest sense: "L.A. trains you to fill out job applications and to write business letters." One hundred and thirty-eight students mentioned everyday survival skills such as understanding prescriptions and recipes. A sizable number thought L.A. would be useful only if a person wanted to be a teacher of L.A., a secretary, or a newscaster. Thirty-four students answered this question with a flat, "It can't." Forty-five students didn't reply.

I challenge you to ask students you know a similar question: "Why do we read?" But don't do it if you haven't first asked yourself—and been able to answer, "Because occasionally I come across a book that knocks my socks off."

Kurt Vonnegut once proposed that anybody running for the school board should be hooked up to a lie detector and made to prove that he'd read a book—all the way through—since graduating from high school. I'd like to propose a similar sort of test for Literature teachers. Ask yourselves, "What piece of literature have you read for the first time in the last year that knocked your socks off?" It is important for your students that you encounter such literature. It is even more important for yourself.

Why Do We Read Literature?

Bruce E. Miller
State University of New York at Buffalo

*T*his chapter is about dedicated readers of literature, and I hope that it will be read by English teachers who themselves love great literature unreservedly. On some other occasion I might be interested in the wearisomely overattested facts that most adults rarely read any book from cover to cover and that the greater part of the minority who do read anything spend their time on how-to books about making money, losing weight, and having sex. But here I am interested only in the true believers in the fine art of literature. They make up a body whose membership, however small it may be relative to the entire population, is absolutely large enough and powerful enough to support roughly three thousand journals mainly or exclusively devoted to the study of literature (I estimate this figure from the Master List of Periodicals in the MLA *Annual Bibliography*, 1987) and to maintain countless literary societies—from the Keats–Shelley Association of America, Inc. to informal book review clubs scattered all over the world.

As with any group drawn together by an important attraction, the members are both like one another and also unlike—like in respect to their devotion to literature, unlike in their personal circumstances of income, education, vocation, and lifestyle. It is what they have in common—more exactly, their reasons for reading literature—that is my subject here. Obviously, some very great good must motivate their reading, since they would not otherwise read as avidly as they do. On the other hand, we know very well that those who do not read literature passionately must acquire the same good in some other way, for candid examination cannot show that readers are conspicuously wiser, happier, or better than nonreaders. By the end of this chapter we may arrive at a resolution of this puzzle, one that will have some implications for pedagogy. Here I shall explore readers' love of literature on the assumption that some invariable purpose at bottom stimulates them all just as a central, defining goal makes a cohesive body of such people, otherwise diverse, as evangelical Christians or democratic socialists. And the assumption of that central purpose makes it possible for the investigation to let a very few subjects or sometimes merely this author's own self stand for the whole group, because what we have in common as ardent readers of literature is also just the one remarkable thing about each of us, the thing that makes us stand out against the general population. One of a pair of gardeners in my townhouse community glanced through my living room window and exclaimed to the other, "He's got a whole friggin' wall full of books!" My fairly modest collection would not strike you as odd, but it astonished the nonreader outside my window.

In "*Ars Poetica*" (1936, p. 409), Horace seems to have expressed once and for all the reasons for reading literature. E. H. Blakeney offers this translation: "The poet's aim is either to profit or to please, or to blend in one the delightful and the useful." These two motives of pleasure and edification have been variously reformulated since. At the beginning of the eighteenth century, in . . . *The Battle of the Books* . . . , Swift (1958) called them "sweetness and light" (p. 235). Early in the nineteenth century Keats repeated the Horatian claim that the great end of poetry is to

be a friend
To sooth the cares, and lift the thoughts of man.
("Sleep and Poetry," 11. 246–247)

A generation later, Matthew Arnold (1960–1977) saw in literature a combination of "the power of intellect and knowledge" and "the power of beauty" (p. 61). And today these conclusions are echoed by the more ordinary lovers of literature whose experience G. Robert Carlsen and Anne Sherrill have caught in their *Voices of Readers* (1988). Readers agree, then, that they go to literature to be delighted and instructed.

As for the pleasure that literature imparts, a less important source of it is sensuous surface, such qualities as assonance, alliteration, the manipulation of tempo, the various evocations of primary sense experience. At this level literature scarcely compares with the other arts in intensity, for it has not the resources for giving immediate pleasure that music, dance, and painting provide through their much more vividly felt qualities of abundant and highly varied pitches and stresses, fully articulated movements, and complex coloring. Schubert involves the listener's ear more than Tennyson, and Fokine and Renoir more captivate the eye than Virginia Woolf or Melville.

But these primary aesthetic qualities of art objects come first only in a chronological and causal sense: They have to appear to us so that we can achieve through them the genuine apprehension of the art object—the poem, painting, or music—and they are the material basis out of which we form our apprehension. These primary qualities are much less important than the illusion which they support and which characterizes that particular art form. Susanne Langer (1953) calls this characteristic illusion a *virtuality*, and describes it as an appearance so powerfully sensed that art appreciators invariably feel it as present even though it is not palpably available for measurement. The principal virtuality of music—time—makes us say of a selection that it is slow or fast, moderate or irregular, even though it has no independent time of its own but necessarily adheres to the common time that governs all things. The characteristic virtuality of painting—space—convinces us that one object in a picture is miles behind another when the actual depth of the work, canvas and all, cannot exceed an inch of thickness. The defining virtuality of poetry and fiction is the illusion of memory, the sense that what we are reading is something that is remembered and not merely invented. Thus the past tense is as appropriate for nearly all fiction and much poetry as the present tense is for most staged drama, where the principal virtuality is the felt presence of a life process.

Obtaining the illusion of virtual memory is a feat for the author, but it also requires intellectual action on the part of the reader, who obviously has to contribute to forming the illusion if it is to exist in any particular evocation. It is here, in the constituting of memory as a virtuality in the experience of the work, that the first really important source of delight in reading literature arises, for we all like to exercise whatever intellectual capacity we possess. Beyond the pleasure we get from using our own minds, we achieve another literary delight through creating the illusion of memory: the enjoyment of vicarious experience or, for short, escape. The dilemma posed by this strange phenomenon is in the word *vicarious*, for how can experience that is yours or Hawthorne's or Shelley's become mine as well? You can certainly give me your ideas or your physical observations, but giving me your experience, which is the apprehending by a particular personality of a particular series of events, is a very different thing. You can readily enough convey to me the facts that you have witnessed, but you cannot loan me your vision and hearing, your intellect and emotion through which I can come to know the facts just as you know them and thereby share your experience.

Thus, on the surface at least, vicarious experience is a contradiction in terms. The word *vicarious* suggests that the thing is shared, but the word *experience* indicates a property that is singularly one's own, incommunicable. As to the possibility of participating in an experience not actually one's own, there can be no doubt, for in reading literature we have all had the sense of *déjà vu*, the sense that what is recorded there has already happened to our own selves. But the difficulty of the logical contradiction remains. The general outlook in some major schools of criticism may afford a resolution. In their different ways, New Criticism, reader response study, and deconstruction all emphasize the anonymity of literary works, the attenuation of the author. Speaking for the New Critics, Wimsatt (1954) stigmatizes as an "intentional fallacy" the notion that literary works encapsulate their author's deliberate meanings. Among reader response critics, Norman Holland (1973) and Stanley Fish (1980) give evidence for the extreme individuality of responses by readers, which seems to imply that each separate reader almost fortuitously constitutes the virtualities of the work, but then both Holland and Fish go on to note regularities of response among different sorts of reader, apparently traceable to some law governing their behavior— "identity themes" in Holland's case, "reading communities" in Fish's. So, for these critics, the virtual memory in the works both is and is not the reader's own. They are the reader's choices (not the author's), but the choices themselves are determined by aspects of personality or environment. The deconstructivist critics also elide the question of who infuses the literary work with virtuality. For these critics, the "hermeneutical circle" never gets closed with a clear understanding of who is the author of meaning and who the receiver. In the view of these critics, language takes on a mind of its own which supersedes both the intention of the author to encode meaning and the determination of the reader to receive it (Tompkins, 1988).

There really does seem to exist a radical difference between the kind of language that is used for communication and the kind which imaginative literature employs. In Roman Jakobson's (1960) widely accepted model of communication, (1) a sender (2) selects signifiers

(3) from a large, public stock in order to indicate a significand (4) to a receiver. Thus, if I write an article that succeeds as communication, I will choose just the words and place them in just the order that will bring to your mind realities which I have already decided to fix there. In contrast to this intentional character of the communication model, literary language seems to be a much more aleatory affair, much more affected by casual circumstances and simple accidents. Commonplace writing becomes memorable through the fortunate intervention of the right editor (*Look Homeward, Angel*) or friend (*The Waste Land*), a subsequent change in a language's genitive inflection ("Here doth lie / Ben Jonson his best piece of poetry" in Jonson's epitaph on his son), or accidents of literary history (the return to wide acceptance of Donne and other metaphysicals in the 1920s). By happy chance all the right incidents came together for Keats to compose "On First Looking into Chapman's Homer" as he walked home late at night from Charles Cowden Clarke's or, again, to produce "To Autumn" during a walk outside Winchester (Gittings, 1968). None of this is to deny that literary language is formed; obviously it is highly wrought. It is, rather, to suggest that this kind of language springs from different sources of creation and addresses different needs in the reader from the language of communication. Many a poet and fictionist at least half believes in the muse, but a good editorialist or scholar trusts to the dictionary and the style book.

The difference of language in the two kinds of writing produces a corresponding difference in readers' responses. In the case of communication, we know very well who is giving the information and who is receiving it. But in literary language this determinate rhetorical relation breaks apart, and we are unclear just what contribution comes from the originator of the language and what from readers, editors, commentators, printers, patrons, and now and then alcohol or drugs. Take the line in which Macbeth (Shakespeare, 1966) accepts the necessity of going on with his oppressive rule:

> I am in blood
> Stepp'd in so far, that, should I wade no more,
> Returning were as tedious as go o'er.
>
> (*III, iv, 136–138*)

Did some commentator originate the notion that this is a broad, slow-moving river of blood and not a dashing stream of water or a stagnant pond? Or does everyone get the same experience out of that passage?

Did Shakespeare invent the "blood . . . go o'er (gore)" connection, or did a printer reduce the length of the line by compressing "go over" to "go o'er," or is this an inappropriate pun which I have gratuitously imposed on the text?

The consequence of this difference in the two kinds of language is that whereas communication conveys a strong impression of ownership, literary language gives no such feeling. The poet "has no identity," said Keats (Rollins, 1958, p. 387). The thing that seems to make vicarious experience possible is the inherently ambiguous nature of artistic virtuality. The memory that fictions and poems impart (and dramas too when they are read rather than acted) is felt only as *a* memory, not as some*one's* memory—not the author's exactly, nor quite the reader's, nor yet the memory of any one of the various middlemen of literature, but just the free-floating, autonomous recollection of some possibilities of living and of their fulfillments and negations. Thus, in a literary work the virtual memory is not anyone's particular possession. All of us, the makers and lovers and ministers of art, have contributed to the experience embodied in the artwork, and so none of us has an exclusive patent on it, and it therefore becomes free to all—not my experience or yours or theirs but just mere experience for anyone to tap into. Art, imaginative literature in particular, remains the most accessible and efficient means that most humans possess for genuinely increasing their experience of life beyond the limits that life itself ordinarily imposes.

In addition to sensuous surface and the vicarious experiences which derive from virtual memory, literature offers another source of pleasure in its form. At least for some readers, intricate verse patterns, shapely plots, commodious expression all enhance their pleasure in literature. Yet it is noticeable that not all readers place much value on formal features. Moreover, different readers make very different estimates of a writer's technical virtuousity. For example, Kingsley Amis (1970) is an accomplished poet as well as a highly successful novelist, whom one would expect to be a reliable judge of another writer's work, and yet Amis flies in the face of the most accepted view and says that John Keats lacked craft as a poet, that a book about Keats' craftsmanship ought to be as short as books on Canadian humorists or Marxist humanitarians (p. 25).

Literature seems to impart two different kinds of instruction, one through direct assertion and the other through vicarious experience. Often readers denigrate direct assertion, calling it didactic, and ridicule such notorious writers of preachy literature as Edward Guest and Taylor Caldwell. But, curiously, readers who happen to agree with the message of a work seem not even to notice that the work is didactic. Certainly the explicitness of the antiwar message of Barbara Garson's *MacBird* offended few persons in the peace movement of the sixties, and E.M. Forster did not compromise his reputation as a superb writer of short stories when he published "The Machine Stops," an emphatic rejection of scientism and totalitarianism. The historical novels of Mary Renault and Gore Vidal vie with more conventional scholarly studies as accurate resurrections of the past.

Still, vicarious experience seems to teach more and also more powerfully than direct assertion. Maxine Greene (1968) suggests that the special power of literature to teach is its alienating us in a beneficial way from our own private and limited life situations, where, because of uncertainties and complexities, only tentative and approximate judgments are possible. A literary work, on the other hand, gives us all the information we need to make definite judgments, especially judgments about character and ethics. In the work, we normally find clear situations which do not require us to act out of self-interest but rather permit us to exercise impartial and ideal standards of right, and so the work is an opportunity for us to clarify values. Such a clarification happened for me in a college freshman English class which I once taught. We had read Hardy's *Mayor of Casterbridge*, and I remarked, merely to introduce discussion and not imagining that there was anything contentious in my comment, that although Michael Henchard was less self-controlled than Farfrae, he was nonetheless much the better man of the two, more magnanimous in the images he entertained of himself and of others. To my surprise, every student in the class dissented. The test of a person's goodness, they pointed out, is the way the person behaves, and Henchard's behavior results in sorrow, Farfrae's in well-being. At the time I thought the difference of opinion was a conflict between sympathetic acceptance on my part and intolerant moralism on theirs, the endless dispute between old liberals and young fogies as Malcolm Cowley used to say. But that difference has teased my mind ever since, and I have gradually come around to my former students' point of view, at least to the extent of thinking that no intention can exist entirely separate from the acts it inspires. So here is a case where vicarious enactment of life allowed me to test my own moral ideas far more rigorously than real life with its obscurities would ever permit.

I think that we have now canvassed the main reasons devoted readers consume literature with passion. Literature delights through sensation, through vicarious experience, and through form; it instructs through authorial commentary and through vicarious experience. But to return to a question adumbrated earlier, why do dedicated readers choose literature when much the greater part of the general population ignores it almost entirely and follows other pursuits? Or, to put it differently, what do readers get out of literature that nonreaders derive from some other source? The answer to this question, I think, has to do with the conception of mind as an incessant activity which, in Langer's phrase (1957, p.44), consists of a "symbolic transformation of experience." Literature, along with the other arts, is one of the great storehouses of presentational symbols, those which project the forms of mental behavior in itself. People who do not fulfill in literature their insatiable need for this kind of symbolization can find other reservoirs. They can go to the other arts, both classic and popular; or they can go to the ritual side of religion and politics. For many others, the study of nature supplies these symbols, and the spectator aspect of sport is still another storehouse. Everyone needs this nourishing supply, some finding it in one place, others in another. Those who read this chapter resort to literature. They could have made a worse choice.

REFERENCES

Amis, K. (1970). *What became of Jane Austen? and other questions*. London: Jonathan Cape.

Arnold, M. (1960–1977). Literature and science. In R. H. Super (Ed.), *Complete prose works* (Vol. 10, pp. 53–73). Ann Arbor: University of Michigan Press.

Carlsen, G. R., & Sherrill, A. (1988). *Voices of readers: How we come to love books*. Urbana, IL: NCTE.

Fish, S. (1980). *Is there a text in this class: The authority of interpretive communities*. Cambridge, MA: Harvard University Press.

Gittings, R. (1968). *John Keats*. London: Heinemann.

Greene, M. (1968). Literature and human understanding. *Journal of Aesthetic Education, 2* (4), 11–22. Reprinted in R. A. Smith, (Ed.) (1971), *Aesthetics and problems of education* (pp. 200–211). Urbana: University of Illinois Press.

Holland, N. (1973). *Poems in persons: An introduction to the psychoanalysis of literature*. New York: Norton.

Horace. (1936). The art of poetry (E. H. Blakeney, Trans.). In C. J. Kraemer, Jr. (Ed.), *The complete works of Horace*. (pp. 397–412). New York: Modern Library.

Jakobson, R. (1960). Closing statement: Linguistics and poetics. In T. A. Sebeok (Ed.), *Style in language* (pp. 350–377). Cambridge, MA: Technology Press of MIT.

Langer, S. K. (1953). *Feeling and form: A theory of art*. New York: Scribner.

Langer, S. K. (1957). *Philosophy in a new key: A study in the symbolism of reason, rite, and art* (3rd ed.). Cambridge, MA: Harvard University Press.

Modern Language Association. (1987). Annual bibliography (Vol. 1). New York: Author.

Rollins, H. E. (Ed.). (1958). *The letters of John Keats* (Vol. 1). Cambridge, MA: Harvard University Press.

Shakespeare, W. (1966). *Macbeth*. In W. J. Craig (Ed.), *The tragedies of Shakespeare*. London: Oxford University Press. (First printed in 1912)

Stillinger, J. (Ed.). (1978). *The poems of John Keats*. Cambridge, MA: Belknap Press.

Swift, J. (1958). *A tale of a tub to which is added the battle of the books and the mechanical operation of the spirit*. Oxford: Clarendon Press.

Tompkins, J. (1988). A short course in post-structuralism. *College English, 50,* 733–747.

Wimsatt, W. K. (1954). *The verbal icon: Studies in the meaning of poetry*. Lexington: University of Kentucky Press.

Answering the Would-Be Censors: Literature as More and Less Than Life

*Peter Medway and
Andrew Stibbs*
University of Leeds

Plato, the Puritans, and many others believed that literature is harmful because it represents (literarily) untrue states of affairs, bad behavior, or at best pleasant deceptions affording irresponsible escape. Though, "unlike the Puritans," Lennard Davis (1987, p. 12) likes novels, he too finds them socially harmful: novels support a myth of individualism which helps modern readers avoid facing the real nature of modern life, and they underpin the oppressive ideology of a fragmented society.

This contrasts with the views of defenders of literature who were influential in introducing English literature into the U.K. school curriculum as a sort of religious study for a secular age. Prominent among these was Matthew Arnold, whose writings on education were edited by F. R. Leavis, who in turn had a decisive influence on the generation of English teachers now in senior positions in U.K. schools. They

31

thought literature (though not, at first, novels) could do good by representing true states of affairs, good behavior, or at worst comfortable possibilities affording harmless reflection. (Some of the more sophisticated—and limited—justifications which have been proposed for literature are summarized by Bogdan, 1985.)

That "good exemplars" argument for literature implicitly concedes its opponents' case, because it invokes the same model of how literature works. Both views, and the wider and more neutral one that reading can both help and harm, treat readings of books as "virtual experiences," closely analogous to actual experiences: They are representations which function as substitutes for the real thing, because the authors have observed the conventions of reporting in order to trap the reader into suspended disbelief. Just as we can "grow" and be made better by exposure to the right experiences, so we can be improved by exposure to "virtual" experiences.

But by the same token, because actual experiences can harm us, so can representations of experiences in books. It will simply be a matter of *which* experiences are represented in the work. The implication of this view is that there is nothing specifically literary about selecting a book for a young person. It is the same sort of judgment parents make in exposing children to certain experiences or keeping them from other experiences—from meeting a particular friend or visiting a particular place.

Books as Things in Themselves, Not Windows or Reflections

Clearly, however, the experiences offered by books are not the same as the experiences they describe. Readers may feel *pity for* a dying character, but they do not feel the same *pain as* the dying character. Nor do they experience pity for a dying fictional character in the same way as for a dying real-life acquaintance.

There are other differences between readings and "real-life" experiences. The most obvious (but most easily forgotten because of familiarity) is that experiences are of life, but readings are of books. Books are objects which we can pick up or lay down, skim or reread at will. They are divided into chapters and they come in covers with title pages and the name of the author to remind us they have been invented. Our "real-life" experience is never determined by others to the extent that our reading, in one sense, is determined by authors.

But neither in another sense do we have such control over "real life" as we can exercise in choosing to shut a book.

Fictional texts resemble normal utterance in form but not in function. A novel may *look* like a corpus of information about a bit of the world, but—with a few exceptions (usually instantly recognized as jokes)—novels contain no footnotes or indices or acknowledgments of sources. If novels don't claim to be informing us, they can't be accused of telling us lies, any more than they can be accused of wounding, soothing, depraving, or uplifting us. A telling objection to Leavisite criticism is that it treats the novel as a demonstration of real-life experience and the experience of the novel as a real-life experience in itself, the moral criterion for both being life-fulness (Eagleton, 1983).

We could strictly argue that literary texts do not "demonstrate" or represent at all, since they are merely systems of signs. They "refer" only to the extent that we conventionally assign connections between the signs and the rest of reality. In this sense a novel is neither a window on the world nor a reflection of the world, but another thing in the world.

However, because of the meanings we invest in the signs—the genres, plots, images, "characters," and words which make up novels—it is not as simple as that. We cannot explain the appeal of the novel only by what it has in common with ingenious mechanisms or abstract designs or as an artful construction which we recognize as creating an illusion of reality. We do experience a novel as a sort of virtual experience.

> Even as we claim that literature does not reflect reality so much as it invites us to make "What-if?" hypotheses about it, we understand that its capacity for engaging the reader in transformation springs from the reader's apprehension of it as something true and real. To deny this is to deny the experience of anyone who has been literally entranced by reading a book. (Bogdan, 1986a, p. 12)

The metaphors of engagement with fiction are powerful—*immerse, lose, devour, transport, identify with*. They are too consistent and common to be dismissed as mere naiveté, and we should all want ourselves and our pupils to go on talking about characters in novels in the same (celebratory, anticipatory, evaluative) ways as we talk about our friends and acquaintances, even though we should also want such talk to be self-aware and accompanied by insights into the constructedness of the self-reflexive sign-systems in which the "characters" feature.

It is also a perceived effect, as well as a declared intention, that some novels and plays do have an effect in the real world by creating representations we take as essentially true—*Uncle Tom's Cabin* and the novels of Dickens did awaken consciences and produce reforms.

Reading as a Dialectic of Rapture and Criticism

We are indebted to Deanne Bogdan for starting us on the line of thought pursued in this chapter. She points out the vulnerability of realist defenses of texts (Bogdan, 1986a), and she argues that a mature reading of a literary (more specifically fictional) text entails an oscillation between two opposed states of relating to the text—an "engagement" with the text, which makes the world it represents matter to us as readers, and an alternating "detachment," which makes us evaluate it and interpret it as a constructed hypothesis (Bogdan, 1986b).

Bogdan's idea of "oscillation" helps us discriminate between engagements which are vulnerable and engagements which serve to power critical readings. Reading by naive readers may seem not far removed from simple absorption in an experience, with far less awareness of the constructedness and the artifice of a book than of its quasi-reality. Such readers may, in a sense, be at the mercy of the representation and harmed in the way the would-be censors fear. For example, there are instances, real and fictional and comic and tragic, of people wastefully or fatally modeling their lives on fictional exemplars, or even of authors modeling their lives on those of their own created characters (Rose, 1985)! Although a switch from engaged to critical reading does not guarantee immunity, readers who have learned, or more to our point have been taught, to recognize the constructedness of texts—to recognize them as sign-systems, games, and hypotheses—are better able to resist what Robert Scholes (1985) has called that *textual power* which the classics of realist fiction most signally and insidiously exercise. Unless we are educated to exercise our critical power over a text, and recognize the dance which it is leading us, even as we fall in with it, it can delude us into believing it is a reflection of the real world and even into seeing reality only within its definitions and frameworks.

Teaching the Literariness of Literature

To teach such a recognition of the literary nature of literature (let the authors look after the rapture), it would help if we introduced students to some texts where the artifice is out in the open—for instance, Vonnegut's and other novels influenced by science fiction, magic realism, and modern European works in translation. Adolescents' tastes in comics, videos, and cult fiction of the *Hitchhiker's Guide to the Galaxy* type suggest they could enjoy such fabulations and meta-fictions.

It would also help if the approaches to fiction which we encourage by the discussion topics or writing we set on novels did not so often implicitly treat the invented worlds and characters of the novels as if they were documentary givens. Although realist novels such as *Lord of the Flies* may seem to resist it, they are susceptible to a reading which deconstructs the text and reconstructs it in different ways to make it do different things.

So, rather than inviting students to map the island or "Write Jack's defense of his conduct to his Headmaster" or "Talk about a time you experienced mass hysteria like that depicted in the novel," teachers might invite them to recognize the text as an ideologically situated artifact—for instance by rewriting an episode in which they, as authors, exchange the physiques but not the personalities of Piggy and Jack; or add two girls to the *dramatis personae*; or write in the persona of a female and even feminist author; or map the decisive forks in the novel and suggest how the text might have proceeded had some other decisions been made.

The theoretical contributions of structuralism, reader-response theories, and poststructuralist criticism (for instance, in introducing such notions as "narrative grammar," Barthes' "codes," and "intertextuality") have filtered into British higher education too late to have influenced most schoolteachers of literature. Insights from them would enhance teachers' repertoires of procedures for provoking intelligent engagement with texts.

Contemporary children may not have read *Coral Island* but their TV experience, and maybe their reading of Enid Blyton, equips even young readers to recognize in *Lord of the Flies* the use of, and addition to, the genre of stories about children isolated from adults. Such recognitions could be developed and explicated by students predicting the course of the plot and justifying their predictions by reference to both the internal evidence of the text and their external knowledge of other, comparable texts.

For readers to know something of the author (against the entailments of practical criticism) and spot the connections between the story and Golding's Navy and all-boys' prep school connections would help them evaluate the text as the invention of a person with purposes, and look critically at the values it embodies rather than take them for granted as part of an uncritical commitment to the "world" of the novel. Students can list what they think would be the most important cruces or themes of the text to readers (including themselves) of different sex, ethnic, or class background, or previous reading experiences. This exposes the part played in a reading of a text by a reader's individuality, culture, and political or religious allegiance.

More traditionally, some examination of the language, imagery, and symbolism of the text would draw a proper, empowering attention to the status of the text as an ingenious, but resistible, artifact. The same applies to an examination of the manipulation of point of view, selecting and sequencing of events, and relation between the durations of events as experienced by characters and readers, so that, for instance, reading-time and narration-time and their distinctiveness from real-time are foregrounded.

And, finally, the realist canon could be supplemented by some of the recent texts in which authors deliberately set out to subvert the ideology of classics by representing their events from the points of view of underlings—as in Leeson's *Silver's Revenge*, Needle's *The Wild Wood*, or—for older students—Jean Rhys' *The Wide Sargasso Sea*.

Hard Cases and Hypotheses

Recognizing the necessarily dual—referential and reflexive— functions of literature does after all pose some particular problems for English teachers. For instance, what should they do about texts of special literary interest and "teachability," the "morals" of which they disapprove (*Lord of the Flies*) or think their employers might (Cormier's *The Chocolate War*)? And what of worthy texts which seem to distort in a good cause, for instance by presenting in a strong positive light people once oppressed and despised by those with power over them, as if women were typically stronger or black people freer than, historically, they have been? What of dystopias, or salutarily frightening visions of a world after a nuclear holocaust?

We see the answers to these particular problems of text selection in emphasizing the nature of novels as hypotheses which can say not only "The world is like this," but also "The world *could* be like this." This characterization of novels depends on both of their contrasting functions—their referential function which links fiction to the real world, and their semiotic function which makes them hypothetical. Novels do not represent the world, but they are propositions about the world. However, these propositions are not abstract aesthetic constructions, and they can move us to desire or hate the states they present. So they can have political effects. By telling fictions about the past, the present, or the future, they can supply utopian visions of possible futures which may guide our actions and choices.

It follows that we should help our students toward a style of reading which switches between an involvement with a pretended reality and an evaluation of the plausibility or desirability of the posited vision; and the evaluation needs to be powered by whatever joy, anxiety, or indignation the novel's rhetorical force gives to the reader's intellectual engagement. To use a phrase from Deanne Bogdan (1986b), we need to put our students both "in and out of love with literature."

How Passionately Critical Reading Provides Teachers with a Rationale for Literature Teaching and a Defense against the Censors

If literature were merely a supplement to experience, then those people who have a right to choose their children's experiences for them would have a right to choose their literature for them. If, however, literature offers hypotheses about experience which can only be appreciated by the mature and sophisticated oscillation between two modes of engagement, two things follow. One is that it is worth studying because young people *need* to consider hypotheses about the world, since it is only from these that they will come to better it.

That provides English teachers with a justification for their material, and a defense against the charge that they are exposing children to experiences their parents would rather they didn't have. Indeed, if children are to learn about the range of possibilities within human experience as part of their preparation for life, they *need* to read about experiences which a parent or teacher would not expose them to in reality.

The other consequence of the need to teach the passionately critical reading for which we have argued is that literature needs teaching by experts who know how the powerful charms of literature work, for good or ill. That provides English teachers with an argument that they know best how to protect children from the dangers of literature-misunderstood-as-experience and how to teach the children to be disarmers for themselves of the magical powers of the texts they need to read.

And when there are powerful people around who wish to censor reading material, it is all the more important that there are teachers who can teach the texts which the censors most dislike.

REFERENCES

Bogdan, D. (1985). The justification question: Why literature? *English Education*, *17*, 238–248.

Bogdan, D. (1986a, June). The censorship of literature texts. Unpublished paper.

Bogdan, D. (1986b, November). *Literary experience as total form: Stasis and dialectic or in and out of love with literature*. Paper presented at the meeting of the National Council of Teachers of English, San Antonio, TX.

Davis, L. J. (1987). *Resisting novels: Ideology and fiction*. London: Methuen.

Eagleton, T. (1983). *Literary theory*: An introduction. Oxford: Blackwell.

Rose, P. (1985). *Parallel lives: Five Victorian marriages*. Harmondsworth: Penguin.

Scholes, R. (1985). *Textual power: Literary theory and the teaching of English*. New Haven, CT: Yale University Press.

Literature and the Ethical Tradition

Arthur N. Applebee

*Center for the Learning and
Teaching of Literature
The University at Albany*

*T*he teaching of literature has always been at the center of concerns about the inculcation of ethical or moral values, a tradition that has much in common with recent calls for renewed emphasis on "cultural literacy" (Hirsch, 1987). I begin this chapter by presenting a capsule history of that ethical tradition, together with some early results from a new study of the content of the literature curriculum. I then use the lessons of history to frame some important issues that schools need to consider as they discuss content and approaches in the teaching of literature.

Early History

The ethical tradition in the teaching of literature is very old, dating back to a time when literacy meant literacy in Latin, and reading instruction began with the *Book of Hours*. (On the history of the teaching of literature, see Applebee, 1974.) This classical tradition was carried over to the vernacular in Europe and brought to America by the first settlers. Their reading text, or primer, consisted of an alphabet, a syllabarium, a creed, a catechism, and a collection of prayers and devotional exercises. (The name *primer* itself, which has carried over into our standard educational vocabulary both as a textbook and as the first few grades of school, arose from the fact that those devo-

This chapter is based on a presentation initially prepared for the Conference on Reading, Writing, and Civic Literacy, St. Louis, MO, September 30–October 1, 1988.

tional exercises began at "prime," or sunrise.) *The New England Primer* (c. 1686), which dominated reading instruction in the United States for some 100 years, followed that familiar form of alphabet and devotional texts combined; one of the most attractive of its pieces is the familiar child's prayer, "Now I lay me down to sleep." Later best-selling reading texts, such as Noah Webster's Blue-Backed Speller and the *McGuffey Readers*, continued the emphasis on moral, if not overtly religious, themes and stressed the importance of reading materials in instilling proper attitudes, correct behavior, and a common Americanism.

The interest and readability of the materials took a clear second place to the proper message in these early texts. Following is a passage drawn from the Blue-Backed Speller, offering advice to young women:

> Be cautious in listening to the addresses of men. Is the suitor addicted to low vices? is he profane? is he a gambler? a tippler? a spendthrift? a haunter of taverns? and, above all, is he a scoffer of religion?—Banish such a man from thy presence, his heart is false, and his hand would lead thee to wretchedness and ruin.

Such were the texts good children read as they learned their ABCs.

These texts, though virtuous, were more didactic than literary. It took the influence of the Romantic poets and critics, with their concern for the power of the Imagination to forestall the ravages and anarchy of industrialization, to give literature *qua* literature a strong moral cachet. As Shelley (1821) put it, "Poetry strengthens the faculty that is the moral nature of man, in the same manner as exercise strengthens a limb." Matthew Arnold, who was a British inspector of schools, became the primary spokesperson for the importance of culture in general, and the poet in particular, as a mainstay of civilization threatened by destruction. As he saw it,

> The future of poetry is immense, because in poetry, where it is worthy of its high destinies, our race, as time goes on, will find an ever surer and surer stay. There is not a creed that is not shaken, not an accredited dogma which is not shown to be questionable, not a received tradition which does not threaten to dissolve. . . . The stronger part of our religion to-day is its unconscious poetry. (Culler, 1961, p. 306)

Arnold's arguments were mustered primarily in support of the classical Greek and Roman texts, but they became part of the rationale for the teaching of vernacular literature, which by 1900 had become a staple part of the curriculum in American schools.

But from the beginning, the emphasis on the ethical values represented by a text carried with it a disturbing undercurrent: If children
learned to be more virtuous through the texts they read, they could
also be led astray if the content were evil. Thus, the overt content of
the texts themselves became a critical concern. As one result, a long
tradition of censorship and suppression of texts runs parallel with the
ethical tradition.

Horace Mann, who did so much to foster public education in
America, was typical of many influential educators when he argued,
for example, that novels should not be taught because their appeal was
to emotion, rather than reason. (In this, he echoes Plato's concerns in
banishing poets from the Republic.) Yale's popular professor William
Lyons Phelps was forced to drop America's first course on the contemporary novel after he introduced it in 1895, because of attacks in the
press. Drama was equally suspect: In 1828, a Boston teacher was
dismissed for reading from one of Shakespeare's plays, and even at the
college level Oberlin refused to allow Shakespeare to be taught in
mixed classes until the 1860s.

The arguments of the Romantic poets and critics provided a justification for appeal to the Imagination rather than to the Intellect, but
they did nothing to alleviate the focus on the "righteousness" of the
message itself. For many educators, the morally good became the
aesthetically beautiful, so much so that by the 1920s a committee of
the National Council of Teachers of English could comfortably attack
"the far reaching and pernicious influence" of "The Charge of the
Light Brigade" (Downing, 1925). (Such attitudes, although usually
well-meaning, are never successful. I suspect Tennyson was never so
eagerly read as when some teachers were trying to remove him from
the curriculum. Certainly the audiences for *The Last Temptation of
Christ* were swollen as attempts to suppress it became more vigorous.)

Problems of censorship became particularly acute in the face of
twentieth-century literature, which often challenged rather than af-
firmed the values of contemporary culture. As long as ethical correct-
ness was the criterion, the aesthetic judgment about such works was
clear. As one professor put it in 1923, writing in the pages of the
official journal of the National Council of Teachers of English:

> If we know anything worth knowing about past literature, we can
> say something sensible and often helpful about that much over-
> praised novel, *Main Street*, or about the blatant productions of the
> Vulgarian School of versifying, headed by Vachel Lindsay, Carl

Sandburg, and a few nondescript immigrants, and sponsored by strong-minded ladies like Harriet Monroe and Amy Lowell. . . . The most noticeable feature of their curious volumes is that they need the services of a delousing station. (Baker, 1923)

Such arguments hardly stemmed the flow of new literature, but the futility of the arguments contributed to the eventual acceptance of the New Criticism, which promulgated structural as well as ethical criteria of literary merit and helped reopen the schools to the writings of contemporary authors. In its application in schools, however, it often did so only by divorcing literature from the demands of living.

Even at the height of the New Criticism, however, literature was never completely removed from its ethical roots. There has always been a strong undercurrent of concern with the development of a common culture and a background of common experiences, reflected most directly in the particular texts chosen for systematic study.

Recent History

The concern with the ethical tradition has been very evident in recent criticisms of the literature curriculum. From one direction, a variety of teachers and scholars have questioned the limited breadth of the traditional canon of literature texts—a canon that reflects primarily white, Anglo-Saxon, male authors. These criticisms began in the 1960s as part of the civil rights and women's movements, but they have continued within the academy itself as a new generation of scholars has sought to legitimate a wider range of critical studies. Schools and publishers have often been responsive to such calls for more broadly representative instructional materials, but the changes that resulted prompted a hostile, conservative reaction. In the most widely purchased critique, E. D. Hirsch (1987) proclaimed the disappearance of "cultural literacy" from American schools. William Bennett (1988), as U.S. Secretary of Education, called similarly for a reassertion of the values of Western culture, arguing the timelessness and importance of the classics. Both Hirsch and Bennett stand firmly within a tradition that goes back directly to Matthew Arnold.

What works are taught clearly represents an important part of the role of literature in the curriculum, and as part of the work of the Literature Center, we have been studying the texts that are actually required in American secondary schools—what is being taught, and to whom. The study has many different parts to it, one of which examined book-length works. Let me share with you some of the still-preliminary results for public secondary schools.

In the spring of 1988, when we gathered our data, the 10 most frequently required books were:

Romeo and Juliet

Macbeth

Huckleberry Finn

To Kill a Mockingbird

Julius Caesar

The Pearl

Scarlet Letter

Of Mice and Men

Lord of the Flies

Hamlet

In spite of the complaints of Hirsch and others, the titles are relatively traditional. Our study was designed to parallel a similar study completed 25 years ago (Anderson, 1964), and the changes are rather minimal: *Of Mice and Men, The Pearl, Lord of the Flies*, and *To Kill a Mockingbird* have made their way up to the top 10; *Silas Marner, Great Expectations*, and *Our Town* have dropped noticeably in rank. All but one of the top 10 have white, Anglo-Saxon, male authors. (And, indeed, the balance does not shift appreciably in the top 20 or top 30.) For female authors, we have simply traded *Silas Marner* for *To Kill a Mockingbird*.

There are some differences between what students in upper and lower tracks are required to read. Shakespeare and Steinbeck lead the list for both groups, but the lower tracks are also likely to be asked to read Hinton (*The Outsiders*), Zindell (*The Pigman*), London (*Call of the Wild*), and Wilder (*Our Town*). The upper tracks, instead, are more likely to read Miller (*Death of a Salesman*), Orwell (*1984*), Hawthorne (*Scarlet Letter*), and Lee (*To Kill a Mockingbird*).

What do such results say about the role of literature in the curriculum? Very little. The top 10 do not a curriculum make, and the selections reported by the schools in our study are marked more by their diversity than their consistency. Such results do suggest, however, that amid whatever changes may have taken place, the curriculum is still anchored in a traditional canon.

Student achievement as reflected in the recent National Assessment of Literature and U.S. History shows a similar pattern (Applebee, Langer, & Mullis, 1987). The assessment itself isn't particularly interesting—it is essentially a multiple-choice test of knowledge of authors, titles, and themes. If we look at the items that most students got right, the list is not dissimilar to the lists of books we have just examined: The best-known topics were drawn from biblical stories, Shakespeare, Dickens, Greek mythology, and children's classics such as "Cinderella" and *Alice in Wonderland*).

Such results are somewhat misleading, however, in their suggestion that "students" are somehow homogeneous in what they know and learn. One of the more interesting (if commonsense) findings in the assessment concerned the extent to which students' knowledge was linked to their interests and backgrounds. In general, students were considerably more knowledgeable about the history and literature of their own race and ethnic group. For example, although black students did much less well than their white peers on assessment items in general, they did much better than white students on questions about literature by or about black people ("I Have a Dream," *Invisible Man*, *Raisin in the Sun*, Langston Hughes, Richard Wright). As one example, 53 percent of black students answered a question about Langston Hughes correctly, compared to 34 percent of white students and 27 percent of Hispanic.

Such patterns of differential achievement raise an interesting and troubling issue: What would patterns of racial and ethnic achievement look like if the content of our tests were dominated by black, Hispanic, Asian, or Native American literatures?

Another problem with the National Assessment, like that with attempts to use the "proper" literature to inculcate the "proper" values and attitudes, is that it neglects what students and teachers do with the books they read: Do they treat them, like the precepts in *The New England Primer*, as statements of truths to be learned and remembered? as vicarious experience to be lived through? or as a stimulus for discussion and debate? (Only in the latter tradition can we avoid problems of censorship by opening troublesome texts for critical discussions and debate.)

The recent history of the teaching of the English language arts has been a history of the teaching of writing. The past 15 years have seen a major realignment in the conventional wisdom about writing instruction, shifting the focus from the final written product toward the processes and strategies that students use in order to give that product a particular shape and form. The implications of process-oriented approaches for the teaching of writing have been dramatic, shifting the balance of instruction away from the teacher as authority toward teacher as guide and mentor, helping the individual student learn to develop and defend his or her own ideas and points of view.

At the same time, the recent history of the teaching of literature has been unremarkable, as the profession has devoted its energy to reformulating the teaching of writing. Like product-oriented approaches to the teaching of writing, literature can of course be taught as a body of specific content, either as factual information such as that in the National Assessment test or more subtly as received interpretations of classical works. The latter is probably the most pervasive approach at present in American classrooms—an approach in which the teacher leads the class, through careful lecture and discussion, toward the interpretation that the teacher holds. Such an approach is certainly very much in keeping with the ethical tradition of literary study, which judged a work by its message, and sought to ensure that only the proper messages were delivered to our nation's young people. But that is a limited view of the kinds of literacy and civic virtues that our young people need, and of the role that literature can play in achieving them. It is certainly a view that bears little relationship to the orientations that many teachers have adopted toward writing instruction.

Lessons from Our Past

What does this brief tour of past and present history have to say as we examine our own programs in literature? There are a few lessons of history that are worth consideration and debate.

1. It is clear that selecting literature because of its message is a dangerous and self-defeating task. The values reflected in literature are diverse, and any given set of choices is likely to be attacked, and eventually censored, by others who disagree with the basis of the choice. Works as diverse as *Webster's Dictionary*, the Bible, *The Merchant of Venice*, *Huckleberry Finn*, and *Catcher in the Rye* have been attacked for their unwholesome influence on our young people and have been withdrawn from libraries and classrooms. Such censorship and suppression is hardly the kind of lesson we want to teach.

2. It is also clear that the literature that dominates the curriculum is still relatively parochial in scope, reflecting the white, male, Western literary tradition and ignoring the many other literatures both of the United States and of the world. The works of minority and women authors, which we could expect to appeal to many of our students, may have made it into the periphery of the curriculum, but they have yet to make it into the center.

3. Finally, it is clear that discussions of issues in the teaching of literature have focused too much on the particular content to the exclusion of the ways in which that content will be taught. Discussions of the teaching of writing, with their emphasis on the development of strategic skills and independent thinking, may offer a good starting place as we try to bring the debates about the teaching of literature back into balance. We can no longer neglect the fact that both the what and the how contribute to the role that literature will play in the lives of our children. Attractive books poorly taught will lose their appeal. Superficial works taught at length will not repay the energy expended on them. More than that, when books are taught well, they will invite exactly the kinds of thoughtful discussion, reflection, and debate that we most need to foster as we lead our young people toward their roles as responsible citizens within our democratic state.

REFERENCES

Anderson, S. (1964). *Between the Grimms and 'The Group.'* Princeton, NJ: Educational Testing Service.

Applebee, Arthur N. (1974). *Tradition and reform in the teaching of English: A history.* Urbana, IL: National Council of Teachers of English.

Applebee, A., Langer, J., & Mullis, I. (1987). *Literature and U.S. history: The instructional experience and factual knowledge of high school juniors.* Princeton, NJ: Educational Testing Service.

Baker, H. T. (1923). The criticism and teaching of contemporary literature. *English Journal 12* (7), 459–463.

Bennett, W. (1988). *American education: Making it work.* Washington, DC: U.S. Department of Education.

Culler, A. D. (Ed.). *The poetry and criticism of Matthew Arnold*. Boston: Houghton Mifflin, 1961.

Downing, E. E. (1925). "What English teachers can do to promote world peace." *English Journal 12* (2), 183–192.

Hirsch, E. D. (1987). *Cultural literacy*. Boston: Houghton Mifflin.

Shelley, P. B. (1821). Defense of poetry. Quoted in D. J. Palmer, *The rise of English studies*. London: Oxford University Press, 1965.

Part Two
METHODS

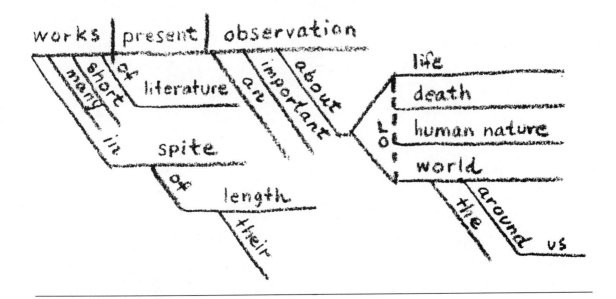

Reading

I stopped at the Cliff's Notes booth at a recent convention. They sell annually, I was told, 500,000 copies of their notes on *Macbeth*. Close behind are *Huck Finn* and *The Scarlet Letter*. So whatever we may think we are doing as teachers of literature, a fair number of our students are reading not the literature itself, but a meta-text. More horrifying still: Cliff (they call him Cliff) has prepared a series of kits for the teacher—each complete with its objective tests and keys to those tests. Perhaps in our last manifestation we will find ourselves teaching from Cliff's notes to Cliff's notes: a field enclosed in solipsism, profitable only to Cliff.

—*Charles Moran*

Silences

Ruth Vinz
Boise State University

Some days I crave silence in the classroom. I'm not talking about a classroom where the teacher's voice is heard often and student silence is honored. I'm talking about silence that allows time for student readers to construct meaning from text. I do not wish to underscore the power of a community of readers, for we all know students learn through dialogue and discussion. No argument. But no matter how fine a class discussion twists and turns around meanings in a literary text, I still search for the marriage of voice and voicelessness in the classroom. Sound and silence are both acts of interpreting and imagining. I've come to believe that we don't give silence a valued place in reader response.

Silence has an uncounterfeitable relationship with thought. Mind has a chance to buckle and bend back on itself, shape and reshape ideas through contemplation. Time with our own developing perceptions keeps us from the stranglehold of too-easy formulation of idea or too-eager willingness to accept solutions. Silence suggests time for fluidity and indeterminacy: both positive strategies for idea formulation. Think of silence as self-talk. Dialogue with self is an important part of the dialogue with a community of readers.

I've considered Bakhtin's philosophy of language, his adamant belief in the social context of language through this lens of sound and silence. Bakhtin's jottings in 1961 evidence his concern with solitariness as detrimental to a developing self:

> I am conscious of myself and become myself only while revealing myself for another, through another, and with the help of another. . . . Separation, dissociation, and enclosure within the self as the main reason for the loss of one's self. Not that which takes place within, but that which takes place on the boundary between one's own and someone else's consciousness . . . (Morton, 1986, p. 33)

I've come to believe in reading literature that the first dialogue, the "place on the boundary" is between reader ("one's own") and writer ("someone else's consciousness"). Later, the larger community of readers opens the dialogue further—after the first silence, but in no less active interchanges.

I've learned much about silence through years of musical training. Rests, I find, hold equal value with notes, chords, tempo, and timbre. Rests extend or emphasize melody lines, offer delays or obscurities— help the aesthetic and technical breathing of a musical score. I find the same operating principles in language when I turn my attention to writing and reading poetry or fine prose. In language, line breaks, stanza breaks, paragraph and chapter breaks, dashes, commas—all are tools of silence.

So, silence is the active partner with sound in music, in language, and I've come to believe it is a valuable reading strategy as well. As I've experimented my way toward a theory of reader response in my high school classroom, I've begun to negotiate the boundary between sound and silence. Such negotiation presents finality, determinancy, and the closing down of developing thought.

Silence gives a teacher dis-ease. We fear it in classrooms. It suggests lack of preparation or engagement on the students' part or lack of expertise to elicit response on the teacher's part. However, silence is not speechlessness. Student and teacher are not struck dumb. Rather, silence gives a sharp edge to thought, time for the mind to enter itself. To engage in silence is a way to break through thought and let it loose. Reader response, at its best, elicits excursions into ideas, the rambling along of the mind with the road map of a text to guide the reader. At times, the best walking stick is silence. On such a journey there is no obligation to follow someone else's line of thinking. The reader explores the terrain of the text through the terrain of her mind. Silence offers a sustained relationship with thought and with text.

I'm reminded that Louise Rosenblatt (1978) describes Barrymore's Hamlet, Gielgud's Hamlet, each demonstrating "the fact that the actor infuses his own voice, his own body . . . —in short his own interpretation—into the words of the text" (p. 13). Not the teacher's interpretation, the class interpretation, or John Potter's (the kid who always has his hand up first) interpretation, but "Does not the reader leaning above the page of Shakespeare's script have to respond to the symbols of the words . . . ?" (Rosenblatt, 1978, p. 13). Yes, Louise. Allow readers to turn the corner of their own imaginings and meet new wonderings before another reader silences the ripening interpretation.

Patience. Interchanges will present challenges for reshaping interpretations later. Thoughts are fragile at first, easily diverted, often misplaced, or sometimes shattered by stronger-willed readers. Rushing thinking processes endangers creation. If we hurry into vocalization, we offer little time to think through ideas, little time to create and represent the text. Then, we may short-circuit the "occupied" reader who, Wolfgang Iser (1974) points out, engages "in the task of working things out for himself, for reading is only a pleasure when it is active and creative" (p. 275).

I like to think of myself in the literature classroom as a designer of occasions. More realistically, I am a juggler of time blocks: time without interruption, time to share perceptions, time to fill gaps or to make new ones, time to generate, time to define, time to redefine, time to construct meaning and explore options, and time for silence.

"What time is it?" I ask. The shuffle of papers, student voices, too loud, next door; the bell rings. So much for rehearsals of the mind. There's always tomorrow.

I've decided time for silence is essential. In what follows, I describe the invitations for silence and classroom life of silences that I've come to believe are essential to reader response. Moments to think. The following procedures might be read as an attempt to work out the dissonance between sound and silence. As I struggle with the boundaries, I find I have more questions than answers.

Where to Begin

That we begin with a story and end by telling the truth is a compelling notion. Laura didn't say much in class discussions, ever. She'd bore her eyes through the text in front of her or write in her notebook while the class discussed. At times I sensed she wanted to shout, "Stop talking." Of course, she didn't, and I didn't understand her lack of participation. She irritated me. Here was a group of 25 bright twelfth-graders sharing their perceptions, frustrations, and questions about literature. Why was Laura detached, preoccupied, seemingly above the talk? She wrote wonderfully reflective essays, short stories, and poems.

During a discussion of *Great Expectations* I called on her. Probably just to get even. Chin on hand, eyes glued to the book, pen poised for jotting, Laura looked up, startled. "Just a minute," she said, her voice steady and firm. "I just realized something connects in all of these hands, and I don't want to lose my train of thought." She put her eyes back on the text and continued with her work.

The whole class had eyes on Laura. They looked at me. I motioned, "Hold on," a slight nod of the head set us all to the silence. We waited an uncomfortable five minutes or more. Laura absorbed herself in her work and didn't notice. The bell rang.

I did some serious thinking through the next class, through lunch, through the long ride home, and into the night. I was startled with the revelation. How could I have overlooked that the classroom agenda had been set by my questions, my leadership in discussions, and the dominant peer voices in the room? We had conspired together, however unwittingly, to set the agenda for other readers. We had not allowed individual readers their own agendas. Laura put me on the track of silence. I needed to reconsider the constraints and restrictions that confine student thinking when powerful voices of teacher and more-vocal peers take control.

The next morning I gave each student a copy of Jon Anderson's poem "The Blue Animals." The poem's brevity, along with the silences in subject and form, raised the issue of silence. We had a long talk about silence that day. Laura entered the discussion. "I need more time to think. It takes think time to piece everything together. If I talk about what I'm thinking early on, it's like I've ended the story and closed it off from my mind." Others began to agree. John said, "I try to show I've done the reading, or that I've had some bright ideas." Susan added, "I always talk right away because I think the teacher likes that. For them it seems to be a way of checking to see if we are prepared." "How," I asked, "can we do this better"?

Respecting Silence

The talk we had in that classroom in the late 1970s was the forerunner for what my students now call "going meta." Metacognition, the detailing of how we carry out our mental work, helps us come to understand the need for silence. The most potent insight, and possibly the most hopeful, is that most students want to support one another's strategies and the diversity of need. In class, we find this involves negotiating sound and silence. For one thing, the teacher's role changes.

The disabling limitation of saying too much too soon can be overcome by one simple gesture. Don't call on the first hand that flies ceilingward. Wait. Allow others room to think. Students are not always comfortable with my silence. No more teacher, teacher questions. No longer do I take full responsibility for a class discussion. I'm not the only class member lecturing, demonstrating, or modeling strategies for reading, thinking, and writing.

I am an active participant in the classroom—talking, asking questions, thinking on paper, participating in group activities, and promoting silence. The class takes responsibility for the potpourri of negotiations—public feedback, sharing, questioning, reflecting, small-group work, and the timing of silences.

Most students make progress at becoming reflective and sensitive to this community of readers. Even in whole-group discussion we are sensitive to silence. As they develop an increasingly sophisticated sense of wait time, think-before-speak time, they become custodians of the discussions. As I step back to observe the overt effects of their respect for silence, the consequences are startling: No one raises a hand in group discussion. Each listens, pauses, gives peers time to think through ideas, and then, after a long wait, one voice will begin. More silence. One or more students may jot a few notes. The others wait. Each watches the eyes, pens, hands, lips of peers. A circle of quiet; each learner looks within. On and on—reflective readers making space for one another. And although the silence is no guarantee that each reader will obtain insight or make meaning, or use the silence to that end, each has the opportunity to shape and pattern and tune the text toward those ends.

Rehearsals of Silence

In the process of implementing this approach, silence takes on definitions, sometimes tangentially, that push the boundaries of connotation but not the spirit of denotation.

We spend time asking questions rather than answering them. Oftentimes, students find their questions greeted by silence. This does not elicit discomfort any longer. On occasion, a student nods, another jots, and a third might attempt a response. No one is uncomfortable when I don't jump in to clarify things with one of my teacher answers. Many times the question remains unanswered, pregnant with idea for further exploration.

In an organized form, we have a round-robin question session. Questions are thrown out one after another—and yes, the pregnant pause between. None are answered. We move through the silence to another question. Questions without answers—a provisional stock taking of interests and concerns—build the momentum of tentativeness.

Certainly writing extends the time for reflection. Students use journals as a way to grapple with their thoughts. Writing time to think with pens is a strategy celebrated in our professional literature and not new to most of us. In a classroom where tentativeness is nurtured, such writing to learn is a potent resource of silence.

Further thinking and reading gave me a key for another type of rehearsal of silence. Think for a moment how you make sense of text: Personal experiences frame the situation in the text; at times, you're struck with the desire to write something of your own; you make connections with other reading you've done; you gather the experience of the text and let it rise up in your imagination in new forms. Literature transforms us into storytellers or poets or essayists or painters. All are rehearsals of the mind. To shape, modify, represent the text in different ways keeps thinking open rather than closing it. The autonomy to choose how to perform the text is an additional type of silence.

In a recent rereading of Umberto Eco's *The Role of the Reader* (1958), I was struck by the similarity of what he describes as a performer's autonomy:

> A number of recent pieces of instrumental music are linked by a common feature: the considerable autonomy left to the individual performer in the way he chooses to play the work. Thus he is not merely free to interpret the composer's instructions following his own discretion . . ., but he must impose his judgment on the form of the piece, as when he decides how long to hold a note or in what order to group the sounds: all this amounts to an act of improvised creation. (p. 47).

I like to think our sensitivity to silence allows student readers to define a work of literature for themselves through their unique perspectives. From inferential walks to ghost chapters (see Eco, 1985, pp. 214–217), students find ways to improvise their thinking about text. Seen in these terms, silence is a strategy that promotes tentativeness, improvisation, and creation.

Refining Silences

I remember very well how pleased I was the day Jason interrupted a peer response session: "Why don't we give ourselves a chance to think? We just keep talking and Julie [the writer whose personal narrative was being discussed] can't possibly have time to think about what we're saying." Jason brought the strategy of silence from the reading to the writing workshop.

Other students keep refining the process as well. "What if the writer doesn't try to explain but just listens?" says Jeff. "Every time we say something, the writer decides to explain. That doesn't mean that's what the writing says. I think the writer needs to stay out of the conversation." Imposed silence. I'm loving their adaptations. In naming silence as a strategy for learning, we've also come to recognize it as a powerful resource in written text. Students recognize the forms of silence—dashes, paragraphs, stanzas, thin poems, fat poems, white space—as potent and potential means for further thought. They recognize the silences a writer creates for the reader. Student writers begin to experiment with such silences in their own pieces of writing:

Across Dakota

Late at night

after
moon lights my pillow
I cross the Dakota plains
back
to a farmhouse
in Wisconsin

the dark, flat, dry summer
when I lay down in warm dust

waited for the train.

Tonia Galdos
Boise High School

In this way, silence extends and transforms and becomes a powerful resource for thought.

Coda

So our conversation ends, and you'll be left with the echoes of words to ponder. Silence, this ugly stepsister of talk, turns out to be a beautiful princess. A text is open for telling and retelling and telling again in those silent moments. A text may wake us up in the night to speculate, to wonder, and to imagine. Silence allows us to keep the dialogue open, to continuously fill in spaces and gaps with imaginings and wonderings, and wanderings. That is the power of not saying too much about a piece of literature.

REFERENCES

Eco, U. (1985). *The role of the reader*. London: Hutchinson.
Iser, W. (1974.) *The implied reader*. Baltimore: The John Hopkins University Press.
Morson, G. (Ed.). (1968). *Bakhtin: Essays and dialogues on his work*. Chicago: University of Chicago Press.
Rosenblatt, L. M. (1978). *The reader, the text, the poem*. Carbondale: Southern Illinois University Press.

Reading Like a Writer

Charles Moran

University of Massachusetts/Amherst

Almost a decade ago, in an article published in *College Composition and Communication*, I argued that teachers of literature should use exercises in what is generally considered "creative" writing to help them in the teaching of literature. I argued for the integration of the three provinces of our profession, "Literature," "Creative Writing," and "Expository Writing," on pedagogical grounds—as a means of bringing students to literature as something more than consumers of culture. What I said then seems even more pertinent now, given two relatively recent developments. The popularity of E. D. Hirsch's *Cultural Literacy* and Alan Bloom's *The Closing of the American Mind* is both cause and sign of a need to treat literature as subject or content, a narrow and ultimately fatal view of the work we do. And our profession's powerful contemporary interest in theory seems to draw us away from, rather than into, the teaching of literature.

In what follows, I offer partial and tentative answers to two questions that seem for the moment to have been taken off the table: Why do we teach literature? and How shall we teach literature? I suggest that one of our goals as teachers of literature should be to help our students become independent, powerful readers. As a means to this end, we need to teach our students to read *like writers*. This is an approach that has been advocated by others (Atwell, Graves and Hansen, Newkirk, Smith), but the work of these teacher-scholars, emanating as it does from the elementary or middle school classroom, has not significantly affected the teaching of literature at the secondary and college levels.

To read like a writer is to understand the writing, the making of the work, at a level so deep that we vicariously participate in its performance. When we read like writers we understand and participate in the writing. We see the choices the writer has made, and we see how the writer has coped with the consequences of those choices. As readers, we write the work as we read. I don't mean here that we create the work as we read, or by our reading, as Iser or Fish or Derrida would have it, though of course we do, in some degree. By "reading like a writer" I mean that as we read we become something like the writer's second skin. We "see" what the writer is doing because we read as writers; we see because we have written ourselves and know the territory, know the feel of it, know some of the moves ourselves. We are informed spectators, real "fans," amateurs who have played the game, know the score.

This goal I advocate may sound a bit belletristic, but as I describe the classroom activities (I deliberately avoid the word *curriculum* here) that would help us all establish, for ourselves and our students, this relationship to literature, it should become clear that a deep understanding of a writer's "moves" is coeval with an understanding of the writer's values—which may, to the reader, then be clearly seen as life-enhancing or otherwise. Admiration is not the only possible response. As the writer writes, the writer makes choices and stands accountable for those choices. As student readers read a work "from the inside" (Moffett, 1968, p. 7), they are encouraged to think critically and to evaluate, even judge, the writer. The aim of this approach is not reverence—and you'll note that I've dropped the fan metaphor here because it may suggest uncritical acceptance—but understanding, a writer's understanding of a fellow writer's work.

The means to this end—this deep, almost emphatic understanding—is the integration of writing assignments into the literature curriculum—and creative writing assignments, writing prompts that cause the student to become not only a writer, but practically *the* writer. Let me move abruptly from theory to application and illustrate this integration in the teaching of Willa Cather's *Death Comes for the Archbishop*. I choose this work because I have taught it (to college sophomores) and speak, therefore, from experience, and because Cather's work is frequently anthologized in American literature texts designed for high school teachers and students.

In teaching *Death Comes for the Archbishop*, my first move is, of course, to read and understand the novel as well as I can. The reading is directed by a question, however: As I read I ask myself, "What does Cather do, characteristically and often? What seems to lie at the center of her work? And what is there that she does that I could legitimately ask my students to do?" My answers to these questions are clearly not absolute or true; they are relative to the way I read, to what I feel I want to teach, and to my sense of what my students can do. My answer in this particular case: Cather often, and at what are important moments in her novel, describes a place, sketches its past, and then connects this place to others distant in space, time, or culture.

Here is Cather doing what I describe in *Death Comes for the Archbishop*:

> About a mile above the village he came upon the water-head, a spring overhung by the sharp-leafed variety of cottonwood called water willow. All about it crowded the oven-shaped hills, nothing to hint of water until it rose miraculously out of the parched and thirsty sea of sand. Some subterranean stream found an outlet here, was released from darkness. The result was grass and trees and flowers and human life; household order and hearths from which the smoke of burning piñon logs rose like incense to Heaven.
>
> . . . The old grandfather had shown him arrow-heads and corroded medals, and a sword hilt, evidently Spanish, that he had found in the earth near the water-head. This spot had been a refuge for humanity long before these Mexicans had come upon it. It was older than history, like those well-heads in his own country where the Roman settlers had set up the image of a river goddess, and later Christian priests had planted a cross.

My second move is to design a writing assignment that will (I hope) cause students themselves to write and, as they do, make some of the same choices Cather made as she wrote. In this case, my assignment was this: "Describe a place, one that you know well, in 25 words or less. Then say what happened there in the past." I give the students this writing task as they are reading Cather's novel, before we discuss it. I don't tell them that the assignment is connected to Cather in any way; indeed, I try to make it as free-standing as possible. The writing is done at the beginning of class and normally takes no more than 10 minutes. No one "finishes"; everyone begins. Here is one student's response:

> At the end of the narrow footpath lie three or four log cabins high on the hill. Children climb up to the top bunks of smoothed wooded planks and pretend they are camping out for the night. Through the dusky light from musket holes in the cabin, the rest of the fort can be seen and tourists now peek in the windows of a nearby makeshift hospital.

> But the last time anyone slept in these small cabins of Jockey Hollow was in the winter of 1777, when Washington and his troops hid in waiting from the British armies and the harsh cold. Almost four hundred men made their camp in this area and hunted for deer in what is now a cross-country path. . . .

And here is another student's response:

> In the middle of the field, just ten yards to the right of the rutted way, lies the first circle. Surrounded by shade trees and tall grasses swaying and whispering in the wind, the round mass of dirt and rocks seemed unnatural. . . .
>
> Several years ago this dirt clearing was a thriving pond, a source of life for the aquatic and plant community. . . .

Once the students have written, I then make my next move: I make their writing the subject of the class, treating it in the same way I will the writing we deem "literature." They will share their writing, reading it aloud. I've even used the blackboard (O, most ancient of devices!) to bring this writing into public view. We'll look at and listen to the ways in which these writers move from present to past. We'll examine the relationship they have established between present and past. I'll not lecture; I'll ask questions. "In the piece that Sarah just read, is the past better or worse than the present?" Or, less specific, "In Sarah's piece, is the past different from the present? or not?" The first student example establishes a child–adult, play–war dichotomy. Now children play; then men made war. The writer seems not to judge—or does she? Are we more at home in the present? the past? Differently "at home" in each? The second student example presents a past that is better than the present—a myth of the golden age—carried in the vocabulary of the wildlife biologist. In the past was a pond, in the present is a bulldozed wasteland. The writer is at home in the past, angry at the present.

I'll ask the writers how it felt to write under the constraints I've imposed. What could they do, and what could they not do? I'll ask leading questions here if I have to. "How many of you included what we could call 'action' or 'plot' in your writing?" "What happened?" Answer, "Not much." "How many of you felt that you were developing a character?" No response. "What's this? Fiction without plot and character? What's left after you've subordinated plot and character?"

And then the final move: the turn to Cather's prose—as that of a fellow writer, not a model. How much is there in her novel that we could call plot? How fully developed are the characters? In the particular passage I've quoted, does she see the past as better than the present? worse than? I'd want to connect the student's piece on the destruction of wildlife habitat with Cather's work: Does Cather include in her view the destruction of Indian culture that has occurred on the ground she chooses to write about? To what extent is her fiction "political"? Would she become "political" if *place* were threatened? Is she more concerned about *place* than she is about *people*? As a writer, which does she give greater value, place or person? landscape or human relationship?

We are now, as I hope you can see, deep in the world of literary criticism, pursuing questions that would suit graduate seminars. One could go on from here to do research into Cather's other work, into what she says about her work, into her life, into other American literature, into other literature by American women, to see how what we've seen in this novel relates to larger contexts. I'm reminded of Bruner (1977) here: "Any subject can be taught effectively in some intellectually honest form to any child at any stage of development" (p. 33).

I have sketched out a five-step process: First the teacher reads and analyzes the work; then, based on this analysis, the teacher creates a writing task designed to cause students to face selected writer problems encountered by the author whose work is the object of study; then the students write; then this writing is read by the class in a way that illuminates the students' own writer-choices; and then the students turn to the work under study, finding differences and common ground.

Let us apply this process to Robert Frost's "Fire and Ice." I choose this poem because it is a real anthology chestnut, because I want to distinguish the way I'm presenting literature from the ways in which anthologies present literature, and because I want to shift genres—from prose fiction to poetry—so that I won't be suggesting that the method I'm advocating is limited to a single genre or "kind" of literature.

I find Frost's poem in a popular and representative anthology; *Reading Literature*, published by McDougall, Littell & Company in 1986 and edited by (ominous sign) "staff of McDougall, Littell & Company." The poem is presented on page 527 rather beautifully, accompanied by a color reproduction of an oil painting. Yet the painting occupies almost half of the page and overpowers the poem. The anthologists seem to assume that the poem needs some visual enhancement, some help from them, perhaps the inevitable assumption of the for-profit textbook publisher. In their efforts to enhance, the anthologists obscure and distract. The poem itself is given hardly more space than the red-inked commentary/assignment in the upper right: "Poets often use symbols to suggest meaning. Read this poem to see how Frost looks at fire and ice."

The textbook writers have done everything in their power, it seems to me, to bury the poem. Beyond this, in the language they use to direct the student's reading, they place the student in the stance of consumer-observer. The student's role, as consumer of poetry, is to "read this poem to see." The questions that follow are predictably text-based and content-directed: "What emotion does the speaker link to fire? What emotion is linked to ice?" Or, under the heading "understanding theme": "The speaker in this poem seems to be simply stating an opinion. Might there be a message or warning in the poem as well? Explain your answer" (p. 528). And the writing exercises are in the genre "literary criticism," where the student is asked to write *about* the poem.

Now let's try it my way, ignoring the artwork, the instructions, and the questions at the end. Let's simply read the poem instead, and ask ourselves as we read, "What is Frost up to here as a writer?" A range of possible answers appears, one that doesn't include the "using symbols" answer supplied by the anthologists. We could look at verse form, because in this case it asks to be looked at. Frost is working within, or creating as he goes, a tight and interesting verse form: nine lines divided by punctuation into two sets of two and one of five. There are three four-syllable lines and six eight-syllable lines: $3/4 = 6/8$. And there are nine lines total: 3, 6, 9. There are three end rhymes: ab aa bcbcb. Two c's, three a's, four b's: 2, 3, 4. There's a marvelous play of numbers here. Interesting that there are no un-paired single units. Is there a seven? And why did Frost not combine the last two four-syllable lines into one eight-syllable line? What difference would such a combination have made to the poem? to the numbers game?

This visible design could lead us to construct a writing task based on form, one in which we asked the writers to take on some of the constraints (but not all, because we want success here, not failure). Kenneth Koch (1970) has had success in leading his young classes through a sestina (p. 216), and Walker Gibson (1956, pp. 298–299) has written powerfully of the virtues of formal/stylistic imitation, the assignment that begins "Write a poem in the manner of . . ." Yet let's not stop here. If we go beyond formal/stylistic imitation, where will it take us? What else is Frost "doing" in the poem? "He is writing a poem about the end of the world." No, that's not quite right. "He has created a voice that wonders how the world will end." Better. Is there something to build on here? Clearly we need to do more than ask our student writers to "write a poem about the end of the world." "Write a poem" asks for too much, in my view, and it gives too little scaffolding.

I'd be tempted to try something like this: "Write two short paragraphs. The first will begin, 'I think the world might end [this way].' The second will begin, 'Or it might end [in this other way].' Ten minutes." With this assignment, we shepherd our student writers more than a little. We make it extremely likely that they will write in the voice of a person who is considering ways in which the world might end. We give them scaffolding: We choose the first person for them, and we give them the subjunctive *might*. With these choices we have precluded the prophetic voice, yet it may be that some of our student writers, given the subject, will move into prophesy in any case. If so, we could connect what they have done with other prophetic writing in the anthology—an excerpt from Martin Luther King's "I Have a Dream," for example.

I'd guess that many of our students here at the university—and we're an increasingly suburban institution—will write about acid rain, the greenhouse effect, nuclear holocaust. Others might choose the AIDS epidemic, ice ages, the death of the sun. Those who really think about the subject will find it a rather heavy one—potentially depressing—but if we worry about this, then we probably shouldn't be teaching this poem (or nearly any other) at all. It may be that the gravity of subject will cause some writers to treat the exercise lightly—and if so, this is an opportunity (1) to look at the ways in which they have distanced the subject, and then (2) turn to Frost's poem and ask, "Has Frost distanced the subject? And if so, how?" This may be the moment to look at the poem's form. How do the two interact—the subject (doomsday) and the contained, playful structure of the poem? Is the poem, finally, depressing? And let's look at the choice I made as a teacher: to ask students to write from an "I think" beginning; and the choice Frost made: to write from a "Some think" beginning. What is the difference between these two modes? How close is the speaker of the poem's first lines to the issue being considered? When the speaker shifts from "some think" to "I," does the apparent distance change?

As in the Cather example, we could move from these questions about the relationship of what we've found here to what we find in

Frost's other works, or other roughly contemporary American poetry. We could look at the way in which another poet, Langston Hughes—whose poem "Harlem" also appears in our anthology—writes about another weighty subject: the deferral of dreams, the fact that some people lead lives circumscribed by race. Is Hughes more direct than Frost? And what do we mean, after all, by *direct*?

When giving examples there is clearly no necessary end, so I must simply make one. I want, however, to make a few observations—annotations, really—before I conclude. The first is that you don't need to be a practicing poet, fiction writer, or playwright to teach in the way I have suggested. I am not any of these myself. What you do need is what Keats termed "negative capability"—that is, the ability to see the writer at work through the writing, to empathize. You should, of course, do the writing assignment yourself. When you do, you'll be better positioned to appreciate how well your student writers have done.

This brings me to my second observation: You do need to appreciate the students' writing, to treat it with respect, as if it were on the same continuum with the work being studied. You can't think of it as inferior to literature. If you do, you will have widened, not narrowed, the distance students perceive between their own work and the work being studied.

A third observation: The approach I have outlined can lead you and your students to general statements about literature, but it doesn't *begin* with them. We begin with a student's writing and move outward from this to others' writing, never losing the connection between what we read and observe about what we read and our own writing. What we learn is, therefore, thoroughly grounded in what we already know. When I teach Samuel Johnson's poetry, we begin to understand aspects of the neoclassical through our own writing. We review our experience and try to frame statements that are true about all of humankind. Then off to Johnson's "The Vanity of Human Wishes," knowing how hard it is to frame such statements, and wondering whether, given our contemporary understanding of cultural diversity, we indeed can. Did Johnson *really* think there was a single "human nature"? Do *we* think so? If so, what is the common ground? And is our common ground wider, or narrower, than Johnson's? Different ground?

A fourth observation: The approach I'm suggesting, the integration of performance into the experience of the student of literature, is one that would seem familiar, even inevitable, to teachers of art or, say, biology. In the world of art education, performance is seen as the road to appreciation (Broudy, 1975, p. 13); in the sciences, we assume that courses should have a laboratory component, in which students "do" science (Bruner, 1977, p. 30). Why does performance so seldom find its way into literature classes? I believe that we'll find the answer in our ancestry: Our forebears taught Latin and Greek so that students could read the Bible; and our ancestors in colonial America were arbiters of taste, custodians of British culture. I don't think the answer lies in any inherent, substantive differences between or among disciplines; that is, I don't think literature is inherently less performative than biology or painting. If I'm right—if we have devalued performance because our ancestors did—then perhaps the reintegration of writing with literature will permit us to get past the stiff constraints of the past.

Finally, I need to say that teaching literature in the way I have outlined has proven to be tremendously rewarding. As Donald Graves and Jane Hansen (1984, pp. 75–76) have suggested, such an approach gives readers authority and helps them engage actively with their reading. What these writers find to be true at the elementary level I find to be so at the college level. Furthermore, as Richard Gebhardt (1988, p. 153) and I have noticed in our college-level literature classes, the "creative" writing seems to bring power and energy to the students' analytic, "expository" writing. It is as if students have made for themselves the connection between "writing" and "writing" that our curriculum tends to obscure.

What is good for our teaching is likely to be good for our profession as well. English, still the most powerful subject in the curriculum, lacks clarity of definition. It seems always to be breaking apart. We divide, separate ourselves, particularly at the secondary and college levels: reading, writing, listening, speaking; English literature, American studies, comparative literature; creative writing, expository writing, freshman writing, technical writing, journalism; ESL, linguistics; speech, film, theater. The approach I outline is centripetal (center-seeking), not centrifugal (center-fleeing). It brings together aspects of our work in complementary, perhaps synergic, relationship. As I think about the teaching of literature, I find myself talking with teachers of creative writing and discovering common ground. I begin to think we should consider ourselves not departments of English but departments of writing, or of language arts. Our colleagues in the elementary schools have thought this all along.

REFERENCES

Atwell, N. (1984, March). Writing and reading literature from the inside out. *Language Arts, 61*, pp. 240–252.

Broudy, H. S. (1975). Arts education as artistic perception. In R. L. Leight, *Philosophers speak of aesthetic experience in education* (pp. 5–16). Danville, IL: Interstate Printers and Publishers.

Bruner, J. S. (1977). *The process of education*. Cambridge, MA: Harvard University Press.

Dewey, J. (1964). *Democracy and education*. New York: Macmillan.

Gebhardt, R. C. (1988, Fall). Fiction writing in literature clases. *Rhetoric Review*, 7, pp. 150–155.

Gibson, W. (1956, February). What the writer teaches. *College English, 18*, pp. 298–300.

Graves, D., & Hansen, J. (1984). The author's chair. In J. M. Jensen (Ed.), *Composing and comprehending* (pp. 69–78). Urbana, IL: NCTE.

Koch, K. (1970). *Wishes, lies, and dreams*. New York: Vintage Books.

Moffett, J. (1968). *Teaching the universe of discourse*. Boston: Houghton Mifflin.

Newkirk, T. (1982). Young writers as critical readers. In T. Newkirk & N. Atwell (Eds.), *Understanding writing* (pp. 106–113). Chelmsford, MA: The Northeast Regional Exchange.

Smith, F. (1984). Reading like a writer. In J. M. Jensen (Ed.), *Composing and comprehending* (pp. 47–56). Urbana, IL: NCTE.

Studying the Harlem Renaissance and *Their Eyes Were Watching God*

Judy Lightfoot
Lakeside School, Seattle, Washington

Schools in an ethnically diverse democracy should be offering literature that springs from a variety of social and cultural groups. But adding a selection of works by nonwhite authors to existing English programs can teach narrowmindedness instead of tolerance and critical thinking. At the school where I work, a secondary school with a predominantly white population, students who study Richard Wright's *Black Boy* or *Native Son* as part of a syllabus of miscellaneous reading in general English courses have sometimes confided to me that such literature makes them uncomfortable, not just because of "white guilt," but because images of life in the books seem to confirm rather than correct racist stereotypes. Black students add personal objections to these books as taught in our existing program. A senior girl told me last year, "Even white students who know better—who know *me*, and know other black people—will say unbelievably ignorant things about us when reading Richard Wright or Toni Morrison. I catch myself wanting to explain, 'My life isn't like that,' and then have to laugh at myself for being defensive. But the books are a problem."

Partly in response to the opinions of students, the English Department at Lakeside recently decided to teach what poet and professor June Jordan has called black literature of affirmation along with literature of protest. This year, for example, tenth-grade teachers will pair one of Wright's books with Zora Neale Hurston's *Their Eyes Were Watching God*, a joyously affirmative American classic neglected until several years ago. But teaching Hurston's novel raises its own problems, and pairing Hurston with Wright (or Ellison, Angelou, or Baldwin) should do more than merely accommodate the disregarded literature of a certain group.

My purpose in teaching the literature of various cultures and subcultures is to foster in students a deeper readiness to understand anything or anyone that is Other. A diverse, multicultural curriculum is in everyone's intellectual interests, not just those who belong to particular ethnic communities. Such a curriculum naturally encourages minds to decenter—to move beyond provincial reactions toward more-inclusive modes of appreciation, whether for alien ideas, unfamiliar persons, or unusual styles of expression. In challenging the existing outlooks of students and compelling them to transcend egocentric frames of reference, such a curriculum helps shake up old categories of perception and requires the continuing mental reorganization we call learning.

However, students can encounter the literature of unfamiliar cultures without feeling a need to restructure their thinking. When they read for universal themes or for mirrorings of personal experience and beliefs, they usually manage to convert alien territory into more-familiar environments. The nursery rhyme claiming that "Everything Miss T eats turns into Miss T" can be applied to everything Miss T reads: she can accept literature uncritically when it seems palatable, and reject it just as uncritically when it does not appeal. So one of my problems in teaching *Their Eyes Were Watching God* is a neat reversal of the problem posed by Wright's books: partly *because* my students can enter easily into the spirit of Hurston's novel, they do not fully appreciate its uniqueness. Their attitude toward Hurston's characters and vision tends to be as simplistic as their attitude toward Wright's narrative worlds, in that students who feel distress when reading Wright's work will typically respond with condescension to Hurston's.

One way of helping students respect the Otherness in a work of literature and acknowledge its complexity while also opening pathways for their understanding of it is to place the work within the context of the culture from which it grew—a culture seen as distinctive, with its own unique combination of political, social, historical, and intellectual circumstances. So I present *Their Eyes Were Watching God* as a cultural creation of the Harlem Renaissance. For the past two years my students have taught themselves and each other about this artistic movement of the American 1920s and about Hurston's life before they begin reading the novel. Appended to this chapter on page 75 is a leaflet of instructions for the project; it consists of background information, assignments, and a bibliography.

My students begin their exploration of the Harlem Renaissance and Hurston's life by reading through the leaflet, discussing it briefly, and choosing topics for research and oral presentation to the class. These topics range from a survey of the Harlem Renaissance as a whole, to discussions of jazz and ragtime, to descriptions of Zora Neale Hurston's childhood in Eatonville, Florida—itself the setting for *Their Eyes Were Watching God*. There is sufficient material relevant to the period and to Hurston's work for a class of more than 30 students to present reports without redundancies. One option—to explain the literary contributions of one of Hurston's contemporaries—opens the work of at least a dozen writers well worth studying, including Langston Hughes, Claude McKay, Nella Larsen, Jean Toomer, and Countee Cullen. Another assignment that can generate half a dozen reports is to discuss some fiction or nonfiction by Hurston other than *Their Eyes Were Watching God*: Hurston was a prolific writer. Two students might collaborate on an especially broad, detailed introduction to the Harlem Renaissance. Three students might divide talks on Harlem music during the 1920s into one on jazz, one on blues, and one on ragtime. Two might share the challenging topic of explaining the controversy among Harlem literati about which language or voice black writers should use, colloquial idioms or formal written English.

The bibliography at the end of my leaflet consists mainly of titles from the library collection at my school. It is a rather arbitrary list, consisting of titles that interest me and that our librarians had already acquired or were willing to add to the shelves. (It seems important to say here that the support of librarians for this project is essential to its success at any secondary school; the staff of the Lakeside library has provided indispensable help, not only acquiring books and setting up reserves, but also helping students with their research.) Some titles in the bibliography refer to excerpts from books not available in our collection, copies of which I was able to make at University of Washington libraries. I keep these copies in a folder in my office and sign them out to students as they need them. Of course, Lakeside's collection has titles not on my list which I expect students to find on their own: social, literary, and political histories of the United States, general reference works, and books by or about individual authors such as Langston Hughes.

I give students a week to do their research before reports begin, and I assign no other homework during that period. We spend class time identifying library resources, pooling good advice about public speaking, and reviewing selected aspects of grammar, mechanics, and usage—a review that becomes especially appropriate at this juncture because discussions of colloquial versus formal expression will be central to our understanding of literary debates among twentieth-century black writers.

Presentations can occupy anywhere from several days to two weeks, depending on the number of students in a class. Besides teaching one another valuable background information for Hurston's novel, students demonstrate some effective approaches to public speaking. A girl giving a history of Harlem brought in a road map of Manhattan to tape to the chalkboard. A boy reporting on Marcus Garvey found a reggae song about Garvey (who was born in Jamaica, land of reggae) and played a cassette recording of the tune at low volume while he spoke. A boy whose father is a Seattle artist brought in slides of Jacob Lawrence's paintings to show the class.

Instead of reading new assignments while presentations go on, students spend homework time refining their research essays and writing informal journal-type papers in response to each day of talks. At least one of my students used journal time to record some independent research on tangential matters. A young man of Chinese ancestry, he searched the library shelves and telephoned the Asian Studies Department at the University of Washington to find out whether an artistic renaissance had ever occurred among Chinese Americans. Though he finally decided that such a renaissance had not taken place, many of his response papers recorded and commented on what he was learning about the history of Chinese immigrants and their descendants in the United States. Other students take the opportunity to reflect on their own prejudices or on personal experiences with prejudice—sometimes ranging away from race and gender issues into feelings about being treated too much like children, or thoughts about their grandparents and how little respect older people are shown in America.

After all reports have been presented, I give students an extra day or two free of other homework so they can complete their folders of response papers and revise and edit their final drafts of the formal research essay, using conventional citations and bibliography forms exemplified in their leaflets. During this time I like to distribute copies of Langston Hughes's poetry for discussion during class sessions, and on the day the folders are due, we watch as much as the period will allow of the PBS "Voices and Visions" videotape on the life and work of Hughes, which acquires considerable resonance from our new knowledge of the Harlem Renaissance and especially from discussions of the jazz and blues that influenced Hughes's poems so strongly. We then begin reading Hurston's novel.

This program of study is especially effective because it is student-centered. Once the talks are under way, the students essentially run the class and teach each other. They take considerable pleasure in exploring a less well traveled area of American literary history and feel they are providing essential information to classmates. They know that I am no expert in the field and that the success of the project depends on the accuracy of their research and the thoughtfulness of their analyses. Although I felt anxious at first about my lack of academic training in this literary area, as I gathered sources and did the reading for the background essay that begins the leaflet, I was able to sketch a sufficiently reassuring mental map of the territory which students would help fill in. Of course, I will grow a little more knowledgeable every time I lead this project, but I plan to cultivate my amateur status, for my lack of scholarly training in the subject helps my students feel they are doing "something real" as they undertake research to inform the class. Teachers who enjoy learning along with their students will find such a project more successful and pleasurable than will teachers who must feel mastery over everything they assign.

This program also makes routine language study more meaningful. Conventions of formal written English become more interesting and debatable as students review the Harlem authors' arguments about effective writing and encounter oral idioms in the literature. Students have strong opinions about whether Hurston should have rendered colloquialisms orthographically instead of in other ways. Students also sense the repercussions of the fact that connotations of words can change over time. They find that black people during the 1920s used the word *Negro* to refer to themselves and one another, but most students realize (and others quickly learn) that although they may need to use the term as part of a passage quoted from their research, they should take pains to phrase their own material more sensitively.

At one time or other during this project, most students express surprise and satisfaction at having studied the Harlem Renaissance and Zora Neale Hurston's life, whether because they see American history or black literature with new eyes or because Hurston's humor, courage, self-esteem, and zest for experience inspire them, not only as black people or as young women, but as persons seeking more vital and meaningful lives. Equally important, the context of the Harlem Renaissance highlights in *Their Eyes Were Watching God* a dignity and artistic integrity that might otherwise be difficult for students to see. Hurston's focus on the lives of uneducated working people and her use of colloquial idioms and dialect eventually make sense to students, not as generically "black" literary strategies—many of her fellow authors wrote differently—but as the deliberate choices of an artist writing out of love for ordinary folk, common folkways, and the language of the streets. In particular, students who have learned that some Harlem artists fought against degrading stereotypes of black people by trying to substitute equally spurious images of perfect black virtue and gentility are impressed by the range and realism of Hurston's cast of characters, who are as subtly complex and infinitely different from one another as are the characters in any masterpiece of Western fiction.

The Harlem Renaissance and Zora Neale Hurston

Some Background to the Harlem Renaissance

At its inception, black art in America was mainly "an affirmation of manhood in the quest of freedom" (Long & Collier, 1985, p. 4). America's first black poet, **Lucy Terry**, wrote a verse account of an Indian raid in 1746. The nation's most famous early black writer, Phillis Wheatley, was born in Senegal, West Africa, sold into slavery, and brought to Boston in 1761 as a small child. Her first major poem was published when she was 17; a book of her poems was published in England in 1773. In early America, **Jupiter Hammon** and **George Moses Horton** were other "writers in bondage"—a tradition, says the *Princeton Encyclopedia of Poetry and Poetics*, "that goes back to Aesop and Terence" (1974, p. 558).

After the Revolutionary War, laws in slave states made it a crime to teach slaves to read and write. Partly because of such laws, most black literature was not written; it was sung, told, and chanted in the form of proverbs, stories, and spirituals and other songs (*Princeton Encyclo-*

pedia, p. 558). Yet some black literature found its way to the page. Some early nineteenth-century writers of note were **Sojourner Truth, William W. Brown, Frederick Douglass, Frances E. Harper,** and **Martin Delaney.** From the Civil War to the end of World War I, black literature focused on the "newly freed citizens" and a "struggle for identity" (Long & Collier, 1985, p. 4). **Albery Whitman, Alice Moore, Charles W. Chesnutt, William S. Braithwaite, Booker T. Washington,** and **W.E.B. DuBois** achieved notice during this time.

The first major black poet of the twentieth century was **Paul Laurence Dunbar,** whose *Collected Poems* was published in 1913. Other authors whose work was published between 1900 and 1920 include **Sterling A. Brown, Angelina W. Grimke, Anne Spencer, Georgia Douglas Johnson, Jessie Redmond Fauset,** and some of the writers who would come to be associated mainly with the Harlem Renaissance: **Jean Toomer, Arna Bontemps, Fenton Johnson, Rudolph Fisher, Countee Cullen, Alain Locke, Nella Larsen, Carter Woodson, Gwendolyn Bennett, Helene Johnson, James Weldon Johnson,** and **William Stanley Braithwaite.**

What was the Harlem Renaissance? According to the *Princeton Encyclopedia*, "A sudden burst of poetic expression in Harlem in the 1920's produced 'more confident self-expression' by black Americans than any of the centuries preceding" (p. 558). The 1922 publication of Jamaica-born **Claude McKay's** novel, *Harlem Shadows*, is said to have sparked this artistic revival, which in turn aroused some lively debates about subjects and styles appropriate to black art. If the life of black people was the artists' chosen subject, would they focus on ordinary working-class folk or on the aspiring middle class? Would they satirize racist stereotyping, idealize black virtues, or present serious portrayals of black life in the tradition of social realism? Was the Harlem writer's imagined audience tolerant or bigoted? Was it white, or black, or both?

Such questions were epitomized in the discussion among these writers of the 1920s about how they should express themselves: in formal written English? or in the folk idioms, oral accents, and colloquial expressions of the black working class? Some early twentieth-century black authors eschewed colloquial expression and wrote formal English. The writings of **James Weldon Johnson** and **William Stanley Braithwaite,** for example, did not contain recognizably "black" idioms; their writings were undistinguishable in voice and expression from literature published by white authors. **Paul Laurence Dunbar,** who grew up in the Midwest, experimented with what he called darky talk, but he naturally spoke and wrote standard English. Other writers, notably **Langston Hughes** and **Zora Neale Hurston**, believed the voices of ordinary street folk should yield the vital idioms of black literature.

Such debates about forms of expression were (and still are) bound up with the struggle of every person to find an identity and a voice within the constraints of the dominant culture's conventional expectations.

Works Cited

Long, R. A., & Collier, E. A. (Eds.). (1985). *Afro-American writing: An anthology of prose & poetry.* University Park: Pennsylvania State University Press.

Princeton encyclopedia of poetry and poetics. (1974). Princeton, NJ: Princeton U Press, pp. 558–559.

Assignments

To create a context for our reading of Zora Neale Hurston's *Their Eyes Were Watching God*, we will collaborate on a study of the Harlem Renaissance. You are to choose one of the following questions or topics and do some research in the area. Prepare a 10–15 minute **oral presentation**. (You'll have a scheduled day assigned to you.) In this presentation you'll be teaching the class something we know little about; plan accordingly. You may want to use the chalkboard for important names, dates, and so forth. You may wish to read aloud short excerpts from selected literature.

After all class presentations are over, you will turn in a five-page **formal research essay** based on your presentation. (But do not read your speech! You must work from notes and communicate with your audience by speaking directly to us.) Append to your research essay a **list of works cited** in proper from—*exactly like* the list that follows the essay, "Some Background to the Harlem Renaissance," which introduces this handout. In the text of your essay, cite within parentheses the sources of information you found in books, and use conventional forms of quotation (again, exactly as in "Some Background . . . ," above).

Along with your formal research essay you will turn in a journal consisting of informal **response papers**. These will be 20-minute responses to your classmates' Harlem Renaissance talks, written nightly after each day of class presentations (except on the night before the day you are scheduled to speak, when you will be busy rehearsing your speech). In your response papers, briefly summarize some interesting information from that day's presentations; then comment on that material. Spend roughly one quarter of your time on summaries and three quarters of your time on responses. Suggestions:

Compare the content of a presentation with a book you've read.

Make a connection with a recent newspaper article.

Compare a personal experience.

Explain what the material means to you.

Relate the material to the subject of your own speech.

In other words, discuss something that interests you from that day's presentations. **Date** each entry, and give each a **title**.

Put these response papers and your formal research essay into a flat **folder** with a **title page** and a **table of contents**. This folder should represent an energetic, independent inquiry into the Harlem Renaissance.

Topics for Talks

1. The Harlem Renaissance: What was it? What writers belonged to the movement, and what famous literary works were published? Give the class a good introductory overview of the period, its persons, and its themes.

2. Harlem of the 1920s was renowned for its music. Bring in some recorded examples of this music to play for us. Describe the origins of jazz, blues, and ragtime, including their source in worksongs, spirituals, and African folk songs. Explain the importance and originality of jazz and other forms of Harlem music.

3. How did American jazz, blues, and ragtime as played during the 1920s and 1930s influence mainstream classical composers? Consider whether and how this music influenced compositions by Gershwin, Debussy, Copland, Bartok, Ravel, or Grofe. Again, play some illustrative recorded samples for the class.

4. Black painters and sculptors flourished during the Harlem Renaissance. Show us pictures of examples of the visual arts of the times, and explain their significance.

5. Though Jacob Lawrence was only a child during the Harlem Renaissance, he was much influenced by the art that developed among black painters of that period. Tell us about Lawrence and his work. Show us photographs of his art.

6. Describe and explain the Great Migration, its causes, and its effects.

7. Summarize the history of Harlem from its beginnings to about 1920. On the chalkboard, show its location on a sketch of Manhattan Island.

8. What was Harlem like during the Harlem Renaissance? Who lived there, who visited there, and why? What was the social, political, intellectual, and literary atmosphere in Harlem then? What did the area look like? Show us some photographs of Harlem buildings or street life. Describe the night life.

9. "A Writer of the Harlem Renaissance": Find the work of a writer other than Zora Neale Hurston and explain its importance. Tell about the author and his or her importance in the period. Read aloud a poem or two or a couple of good illustrative passages, and discuss their significance.

10. Explain the controversy during the Harlem Renaissance about what language or voice black writers "ought to" write in. Present the opposing views of the two groups of black writers, and clarify their reasoning. What was Hurston's view of the issue? What is yours? (Go beyond "Everyone has a right to write in whatever way he or she chooses" or "If writers want to sell, they just have to offer potential buyers what they want to read." As the background essay at the start of this leaflet suggests, the issue is not so simple.)

11. Marcus Garvey was an influential figure of the Harlem Renaissance. Explain Garvey's ideas about black politics and American society in the early twentieth century. Assess his influence.

12. Booker T. Washington, who lived before the Harlem Renaissance, is the subject of a brief but significant quarrel in the last part of *Their Eyes Were Watching God*. Summarize

Washington's life and his ideas about how racial problems in the United States could gradually be solved.

13. Describe Zora Neale Hurston's childhood in Eatonville, Florida. Mention influential people, places, and events. Describe the special qualities of the girl Zora.

14. Describe Hurston's life in Harlem, giving us a vivid appreciation of her character and of the impression she made on friends and acquaintances. Cite memorable incidents, images, and conversations. Show us pictures of Hurston.

15. Where, when, why, and how did Hurston study anthropology? What did she learn about her people's folkways and arts? What did she come to value in these?

16. Choose a story, article, essay, or excerpt by Hurston (not part of *Their Eyes Were Watching God*). Summarize the reading well and succinctly, quote excerpts where interesting and appropriate, and respond to the selection.

17. Briefly, who is Alice Walker? What is Walker's opinion of Hurston and her work? Why does Walker say that knowledge of Hurston is important to writers like her? Succinctly and vividly tell the story of Walker's search for Hurston's grave.

18. Poet June Jordan was influenced by Hurston. Briefly, who is June Jordan? Read her article on Hurston and Richard Wright, and explain her views to the class. Choose a poem or two of Jordan's to read aloud with comment. (Jordan has a thought-provoking poem for readers of *Native Son*: "Richard Wright was Wrong.") Does Jordan's poetry seem to you more like Wright's (as Jordan describes it in her article from *Black World*) or more like Hurston's as she describes it in that article?

19. Read a story by Mark Twain, Ring Lardner, Eudora Welty, Flannery O'Connor, or another white author who uses colloquial idioms or dialect. Choose an interesting passage of dialect or colloquial speech, and translate the passage into formal written English. For your presentation, give a brief background for the author and explain why he or she used colloquial idioms in this work. Then summarize the story from which your excerpt is taken. Read your dialect passage and your formal translation aloud for comparison, then your dialect passage again. Explain what is lost in translating the

dialect or the colloquial idioms into formal written English. Is anything gained? Taking into account earlier talks, summarize what the class has learned about the purposes and effects of writing in oral idioms.

Bibliography

Anderson, J. (1981). That was New York: Harlem. *The New Yorker. A history of New York in four parts as follows*:

June 29, 1981: Harlem 1890–1920. The Great Migration: black people move to Harlem (pp. 38–44); life in Harlem (pp. 44–59); stage musicals in and from Harlem (pp. 59–65); Paul Laurence Dunbar (pp. 62–65); conflicts between whites and blacks (pp. 65–69).

July 6, 1981: Harlem before, during, and after World War I. Life in Harlem just prior to WWI (pp. 55–67); jazz and other music, Ellington, Joplin, etc. (pp. 61–64); feelings about skin color (pp. 64–66); black soldiers fight in WWI (pp. 67–72); life in Harlem (pp. 75–77); Marcus Garvey (pp. 77–82); music (pp. 82–85).

July 13, 1981: Harlem in the 1920s. Life in Harlem (pp. 38–79); Prohibition (pp. 41–46); playing the "numbers" (pp. 46–47); rent parties (pp. 47–52); night life, music, the Cotton Club, etc. (pp. 52–64); politics (pp. 64–68); the Harlem Renaissance (pp. 68–79).

July 20, 1981: Harlem 1929 and after; the Great Depression. Music (pp. 43–47); devastating effects of the Depression (pp. 47–53); Father Divine, G. W. Benton, and Harlem churches (pp. 49–60); art and theater (pp. 60–66); racial conflicts and riots in Harlem (pp. 68–70); music (pp. 70–71); Harlem society (pp. 71–76); list of famous names of the period (pp. 76–77).

Anderson, J. (1983). *This was Harlem.* New York: Farrar Straus Giroux. *This volume includes the material from* The New Yorker *articles listed above.*

Aptheker, H. (1973). *Afro-American history: The modern era.* Secausus, NJ: Citadel.

Baker, H. A. (1987). *Modernism and the Harlem Renaissance.* Chicago: University of Chicago Press. *A scholarly, challenging book—probably unsuited to secondary students, but useful for teachers.*

Bell, B. W. (1987). *The Afro-American novel and its tradition.* Amherst: University of Massachusetts Press.

Bontemps, A. (1972). *The Harlem Renaissance remembered.* New York: Dodd Mead. *A memoir and an anthology of writings from the period.*

Chapman, A. (1968). *Black voices.* New York: New American Library. *Literary anthology.*

Clarke, J. H. (Ed.). (1974). *Marcus Garvey and the vision of Africa*. New York: Random.

Cooper, W. F. (1987). *Claude McKay: Rebel Sojourner in the Harlem Renaissance*. Baton Rouge: Louisiana State University Press. *Biography and criticism*.

Cronon, E. D. (1969). *The story of Marcus Garvey*. Madison: University of Wisconsin Press.

Fleming, R. E. (1987). *James Weldon Johnson*. Boston: Twayne. *Biography and criticism*.

Gates, H. L., Jr. (1985, June 21). A Negro way of saying. *New York Times Book Review*, p. 1. *A review of some of Hurston's work*.

Gates, H. L., Jr. (1986). *Figures in black: Words, signs, and the racial self*. New York: Oxford University Press. *A scholarly analysis of the language of black literature*.

Harlem Renaissance: Art of black America. (1987). New York: Harry N. Abrams.

Hemenway, R. (1977). *Zora Neale Hurston: A literary biography*. Urbana: University of Illinois.

Huggins, N. (1971). *The Harlem Renaissance*. New York: Oxford University Press. *Literary history and criticism*.

Hughes, L. (1986). *The big sea: An autobiography*. New York: Thunder's Mouth Press. *Reminiscences*.

Hull, G. T. (1987). *Color, sex, and poetry: 3 women writers of the Harlem Renaissance*. Bloomington: Indiana University Press.

Hurst, F. (1986). A personality sketch. In H. Bloom (Ed.), *Zora Neale Hurston* (pp. 21–24). New York: Chelsea House. *Memoir: Hurston was employed for a time as a secretary to Miss Hurst*.

Hurston, Z. N. (1967). *Moses, man of the mountain*. Urbana: University of Illinois Press. *Novel*.

Hurston, Z. N. (1978). *Mules and men*. Bloomington: Indiana University Press. *Some of Hurston's studies in anthropology*.

Hurston, Z. N. (1979). *I love myself when I am laughing . . . and then again when I am looking mean and impressive: A Zora Neale Hurston reader*. New York: The Feminist Press. *Alice Walker wrote the dedicatory essay for this volume. "On Refusing to Be Humbled by Second Place in a Contest You Did Not Design," a tribute to Hurston*.

Hurston, Z. N. (1984). *Dust tracks on a road: An autobiography*. Urbana: University of Illinois Press.

Hymes, D. (1974). *Reinventing anthropology*. New York: Vintage. *Discussions of theories behind anthropological approaches such as Hurston's*.

Jordan, J. (1974, August). On Zora Neale Hurston and Richard Wright. *Black World, 23*, pp. 4–8.

Jordan, J. (1980). *Passion: New poems, 1977–1980*. Boston: Beacon.

Jordan, J. (1985a). The difficult miracle of black poetry in America, or, something like a sonnet for Phillis Wheatley. In *On Call: Political Essays* (pp. 87–98). Boston: South End Press. *A critique of Wheatley's use of formal English idioms; Jordan explains why some black writers "wrote white."*

Jordan, J. (1985b). *Living room*. New York: Thunder's Mouth Press. *Poems.*

Jordan, J. (1985c). Nobody mean more to me than you and the future life of Willie Jordan. In *On Call: Political Essays* (pp. 129–139). Boston: South End Press. *Jordan describes the lessons in black English she gives her university students.*

Long, R. A., & Collier, E. A. (Eds.). (1985). *Afro-American writing: An anthology of prose & poetry*. University Park: Pennsylvania State University Press.

Margolies, E. (Ed.). (1970). *A native sons reader*. New York: Lippincott. *Literary anthology.*

Rampersad, A. (1986). *The life of Langston Hughes*. 2 vols. New York: Oxford University Press.

Ryan, W. F. (1988, December). Blackening the language. *American Visions*, pp. 32–37.

Singh, A. (1976). *The novels of the Harlem Renaissance: Twelve black writers, 1923–1933*. University Park: Pennsylvania State University Press.

Walker, A. (1983). *In search of our mothers' gardens*. New York: Harcourt Brace. *This book contains two essays about Hurston: "Zora Neale Hurston: A Cautionary Tale and a Partisan View" and "Looking for Zora."*

Washington, M. H. (Ed.). (1987). *Invented lives: Narratives of black women 1860–1960*. New York: Doubleday.

Wheat, E. (1986). *Jacob Lawrence: American painter*. Seattle: University of Washington Press.

Wideman, J. (1988, January 24). The black writer and the magic of the word. *New York Times Book Review*, p. 1.

Responding

The evangelical movement of reader response is in high gear. Converts are won daily. Even the textbook companies claim to have reader-response models integrated in their Adventuring through Literature series. If we look at the thin veneer of reader response in such textbooks, we see the dangers of labeling without understanding. These series follow a traditional "read and answer the questions" model. The questions may appear to elicit a wider range of responses or ask students to respond in more imaginative ways, but the text still provides a voice of authority, assuming knowledge of what the selection contains that is worthy of study.

—Dan Kirby and Ruth Vinz
(This excerpt is from "Landscapes of the Imagination," which will appear in the next *Vital Signs*)

An Agenda for a Reading–Writing File

Bill Corcoran
James Cook University of North Queensland

*T*he origins of the ideas that follow are far from abstruse. They derive particularly from some basic propositions in reader-response theory and cultural criticism. They acknowledge, for example, that meaning is made in the interface of a transaction between text and reader, or between emergent text and writer. They acknowledge, as well, that literary texts contain an ideology—a set of cultural attitudes, assumptions, and beliefs that readers can argue with, and which the writer may not even have been aware of. In addition to proposing a method for tying together most of the reading and writing that students do over the complete span of a semester or a year, I want particularly to open the way for students to become both reflexive and resistant readers and writers. In essence, the agenda outlined in this chapter provides a list of specific activities intended to illustrate how a reading–writing classroom incorporates the following continuities and characteristics:

1. The capturing of initial responses to literature through the use of structured and unstructured journal and reading log entries.

2. Illustrations of how initial responses are changed, modified, and extended through structured questions that take account of the literary and cultural repertoires of both students and texts.

3. Collaborative explorations of the pragmatic and framing contexts that constitute the connections between and necessary conditions for reading and writing.

4. The provision of frequent opportunities for self-conscious (reflexive) analysis of cognitive and cultural reading strategies.

5. The establishment of culturally conscious ways of reading and writing texts and understanding textuality.

6. The documenting of students' attempts at resistant or strong readings as they read against the grain of dominant literary or cultural text strategies.

7. The provision of frequent opportunities for the student-writer to become a reader composite (a multiple "reading voice") that questions the ideational and interpersonal elements of an emergent social text.

8. Explorations of the role of models, especially literary ones, in the development of students' writing.

9. The provision of opportunities for students to engage in some experimental writing based on rereadings of generic conventions.

Taken as a whole, these strategies signal an attempt to marry elements of reader-response theory, cultural criticism, and cognitive process approaches to writing. There is an acknowledgment, first, that reader-response approaches have been particularly helpful in charting a phenomenology of reading, in specifying what a skilled reader does under the impress of the quite specific forms of textual instruction that mark out the literary text. What Iser (1978), Rosenblatt (1978), Fish (1980), and others have taught us is how to use strategies such as interrupted readings; cloze procedures, or deletions at the level of the word, sentence, or paragraph; or the sequencing of a scrambled text to draw attention to such reader-like activities as picturing, anticipating, and retrospecting, or to specific aspects of the text's construction (See Corcoran and Evans, 1987). What they are less successful at is helping us understand how, as potential readers and writers, we have been culturally constructed by the reading and writing we have already done. A cultural theory of literary production (Barthes, 1974; Culler, 1983; Scholes, 1985) would argue that the sort of reader or writer any of us can ever hope to become will depend on our understanding of the ideology of text. We need, therefore, to be both *active* and *resistant* readers in order to understand how what is coded in literature as ideological content will be unequally distributed, and distinguished along gender, race, class, and other power-laden cultural axes.

What I have in mind is a ring binder divided, for convenience and for significant theoretical reasons, into three discrete sections. Part A will provide space for those immediate encounters with the text that acknowledge the primacy of the earliest moments of the reader–text transaction. Part B will provide opportunities for a series of later reflections and analyses that allow the reader to consider in more exacting detail not only those textual and personal elements that were responsible for the initial response, but also those later modifications of response forged in the social context of the classroom. Part C will constitute a repository of models and experiments that act as tangible evidence of the ways in which the self-conscious reading and rewriting of text enfranchises the reader as writer and the writer as reader. Let us look, then, in more detail at a range of activities that could be used to fulfil the purposes of each of these sections.

Part A: Initial Encounters and Jottings

1. *Personal jottings:* This involves exploratory or expressive writing, using notes and annotations, or immediate unstructured response statements that acknowledge students' need for meaning space.
2. *Reading logs* or *journals*: These are used for prediction and retrospection activities while reading any extended narrative. Entries could be made after the opening chapter, before or after a narrative break or gap, before or after a change of narrator, just after any significant revelation, or just before the ending.
3. *The framing of personal or group questions* seems essential if students are to become active interrogators of texts.
4. The procedure of using a *double-entry notebook* allows students to reflect on the place of their own memories, speculations, and analogies. The form, as Berthoff (1981) and others have indicated, could be as follows:

WHAT HAPPENS	WHAT HAPPENS TO ME
Characters	I remember when . . . That's the
Events	way things are . . . What if? . . .
Places and contexts	Suppose that . . . I wonder why . . .
Themes and issues	I realize now . . .

5. *Drawing* initial responses.

6. Initial *cultural perspectives*: List in two columns those aspects of your own constructed perspective (e.g., of sex, family and social background, age difference, historical placement) that are *helpful* to the reading and those that *hinder* the reading.

7. *Marking the text like a structuralist*: Underline with straight or squiggly lines bits of the text that deal with one thing rather than another. Identify patterns, connections, or oppositions that seem to be in the text.

8. *Tampering with textual elements*: As a way in to particular texts the teacher uses cloze or sequencing activities to draw attention to textual construction at the level of the word, sentence, paragraph, or stanza.

9. *Responding to statements*: The teacher or a small group of students develops six or seven statements or propositions that act as intended effects on the reader ("The story was written to shock you."), or as possible authorial or textual intentions ("The story was written to show . . ."). Students then mark the three most important statements as frames for immediate responses, and the raw material for later reflections and analysis.

Part B: Later Reflections and Analysis

1. *Refining visual responses*: Students work on their initial drawings or charts at a more artistic or polished level.

2. *Response graphs*: These can be used to track degrees of reader involvement with the text, or the rising and falling fortunes of major characters.

3. *Working on chapters and story construction*: Tabulate all changes of scene, time, place, narrator, or perspective. Provide titles for chapters or identify the function of chapters or chapter breaks such as problem setting, laying false clues, creating suspense, scene changing. Do chapter endings have stylistic patterns similar to those of chapter beginnings? Does the first sentence of the next chapter follow from the last sentence of the previous chapter?

4. *Segmenting a story or poem*: This open invitation to break the story or poem into as many or as few sections as one likes pays regard to issues as various as plots and subplots, character relationships, changes of mood, setting or narrator, or structural issues related to genre such as the formulaic patterns of romance, crime, or science fiction stories.

5. *Transparent narration*: The purpose of this activity is to identify narrative strategies, and to consider how particular narrative stances could be altered. In most cases, for example, changes in tense, perspective, or persona will invariably alter the text's ideology.

6. *Transparent description*: Are the descriptive sections separate or interwoven, or is there very little description? *Who* is providing the descriptions? Is there anybody else in a position to provide this description? How and why would his or her description be different? How, inevitably, are descriptions colored by the ideology or emotional states of the persons presenting them?

7. *Character functions and reversals*: Attention can be drawn to the ways in which characters are constructed in language shared in common by author and reader by the listing of words used to describe characters, of points at which there are significant changes in character, or of character qualities at the *start* or *end* of longer pieces of fiction. Consider, particularly, what changes would be made to the novel or story if the sex, social class, or race of particular characters were changed.

8. *Genres and reading strategies or practices*: Students constantly should be encouraged to reflect on the genre they think a particular text belongs to, to indicate the point at which they recognize the text as belonging to that genre, and

to carefully consider the nature of any departures from generic conventions. These entries should eventually shed some light on the strategies students use in reading across adjacent genres such as fairy stories and fables, or science fiction and realistic fiction.

9. *Metacognitive comments on textuality*: The question for exploration here is how students learn to read novels (like Aidan Chambers' *Breaktime*) that act out in the text certain strategies of reading by constantly juxtaposing a range of text types.

10. *Notes on active and resistant readings*: Using an adapted version of Bleich's (1975) response heuristic, and Probst's (1988) "Dialogue with a Text," the two levels of questions indicated below are an attempt to marry *reader* and *cultural* versions of response theory.

Feelings:
(a) What feelings did the text awaken in you? What emotions did you feel as you read the text?
(b) How are these feelings and emotions related to your age, sex, family background, prejudices, and so on? Why would you *expect* to react in that way?

Perceptions:
(a) What did you see happening in the text? Paraphrase it— retell the major events briefly.
(b) Were there particular things left out that made the text difficult to understand? What other information would you have wished the writer had given you?

Associations:
(a) What memories does the text call to mind—of people, places, events, sights, smells, or of something even more ambiguous, perhaps feelings or attitudes?
(b) What aspects of your own background produced these memories, associations, or attitudes? Is there something quite clearly related to your sex, race, or class background that is making this memory strong for you?

Thoughts, ideas:
(a) What thoughts or ideas were suggested by the text? Explain them briefly.

(b) How are these thoughts and ideas related to your own society or culture? Do you think the text gives a *fair* interpretation of these ideas?

Selection of textual elements:
(a) On what, in the text, did you focus most intently as you read—what word, phrase, image, or idea?
(b) Did this dominant word or phrase narrow your reading? On a second or third reading, can you see any equally important (or perhaps opposite) words, phrases, or images?

Identification of problems:
(a) What is the most difficult word in the text?
(b) What is there in the text, or in your own reading, that you have most trouble understanding?

Patterns of response:
(a) How did you respond to the text—emotionally or intellectually? Did you generally feel involved with the text, or distant from it?
(b) At what particular points in the text did you find it difficult to read? What particular parts of the text did you find challenging, exciting, or boring and remote from your experience?

Other readings:
(a) How did your reading of the text differ from those of other members of your group?
(b) Which of the readings in your group provides the most challenge? Why?

Intertextual associations:
(a) Does this text call to mind any other work (poem, play, film, story) you have read recently?
(b) What are the particular textual features that connect the two works?

Part C: Writing from Reading: Models and Experiments

This section of the file contains all of the text models used in class, together with student-selected texts which might act as catalysts for writing initiated by the student. A catalogue of models and experiments in this version of what used to be called a "commonplace book" might include the following:

1. *Imitation* or writing in the style of. (Dialogue after Hemingway; memories like Laurie Lee's; characters like Dylan Thomas's.)

2. *Writing A in the style of B.* (Harlequin romances as Emily Bronte; Bruce Dawe as Alexander Pope; a Western in the form of a football commentary.)

3. *Rewriting* scenes, incidents, chapters, endings *from various points of view*. A particularly important element here is the selection of minor or marginalized characters in order to see whose meanings or significances have been suppressed and whose valorized or privileged.

4. *Transforming/reworking in a different form or genre.* (Poems as newspaper reports, anecdotes, or dramatized dialogue; chapters of novels as radio scripts; a suspense or ghost story as a romance.)

5. *Formula writing* based on conventional structures. (Crime stories; situation comedies; romances; science fiction.)

6. *Experimental writing* involving deliberate manipulation of conventional text strategies. (*In medias res* narration; elliptical plotting; indeterminate endings; unreliable narration; stories told entirely in dialogue.)

7. *Textual pastiche.* Generating stories that contain a required list of text types. (Journalistic prose; encyclopedia extracts; letters; diary entries; limericks; Woody Allen riddling; a political speech; a passage from an instruction manual.)

8. *Adding* or *inserting* additional episodes or chapters. (Smuggling an additional, undetected conversation into *Catch 22* or *The Grapes of Wrath*; *Mansfield Parsonage*, the later life of Fanny and Edmund; *Jane*, with Jane Fairfax instead of Emma at the center; *Inspector Bucket Solves the Mystery*, giving the character from *Bleak House* the Sherlock Holmes treatment.)

9. *Providing missing incidents* or *documents* implied or referred to in the text. (Fanny Price's diary entries in *Mansfield Park*; David Copperfield writing home from Yarmouth; pages from Inspector Bucket's notebook.)

10. *Shifting the medium*. Public scenes, such as the acquittal of Aziz, the conviction of Tom Robinson framed for different media (the next day's newspaper, a radio report, a letter from an eyewitness), but with particular emphasis on *audience* and *genre* features.

11. *Modernizing*. Something more than artificial paraphrase is envisaged here as passages from older texts are brought forward so that the assumptions and ideology embedded in the original and rewritten language reveals something about the constructed nature of characters and events. (How, in the latter part of the twentieth century, might a Mr. Elton propose to Emma? How might Jane Eyre suffer at a modern Lowood school?)

12. *Symptomatic reading and rewriting*. Read any historically distanced play, poem, story, or video clip so that the *absences* in the text are foregrounded. (Recasting a seventeenth-century love poem with a dominant female and a submissive male; rewriting Blake's "London" from the point of a twentieth-century tourist.)

13. *Contextualizing I*. What changes are in evidence from the earlier "drafts" produced by major writers? (From Joyce's "epiphanies" notebook and earlier sketches to *Dubliners*; from Lawrence's short stories and poems to *Sons and Lovers*.)

14. *Contextualizing II*. Using historical research to present a documentary of original sources and commentary to a group about to read a particular text. Suggested forms of documentation include any texts or artifacts responsible for the cultural framing or the literary and cultural repertoires of the implied reader. (Maps; historical documents; letters; diaries; contemporary reviews; pictures, photographs, or paintings.)

15. *Contextualizing III*. Employing useful intertextual references. (Reading du Maurier's *Rebecca* before turning to *Jane Eyre* or *The Turn of the Screw*; tracing the changes in a narrative through various genres as Isherwood's *Goodbye to Berlin* becomes a play, *I Am a Camera*, then a musical, and finally a film, (*Cabaret*.)

Undoubtedly, teachers will add to this list of possible reading–writing connections. For the moment, it seems important to engage in some careful documentation of the ways in which the evidence of the proposed reading–writing file might make the teaching of *both* reading and writing less haphazard and disconnected. The agenda is replete with suggestions for rethinking the relationships between literature and original or creative writing. Indeed, Scholes (1982) sums up much of the hidden agenda when he argues the need for focused forms of teacher intervention:

> We read as we have been taught to read and until we have been taught to look for certain things we will not see them. And we write—always and inevitably—on the basis of models of writing we have already encountered. The ability to be "creative" is not given to the novice but is earned by mastering the conventions to the point where improvisation becomes possible, and power finally is exchanged for freedom once again. (p. 6)

REFERENCES

Barthes, R. (1974). S/Z. Trans. R. Miller. New York: Hill & Wang.

Berthoff, A. (1981). *The making of meaning.* Portsmouth, NH: Boynton/Cook.

Bleich, D. (1975). *Readings and feelings: An introduction to subjective criticism.* Urbana, IL. NCTE.

Corcoran, B. & Evans, E. (Eds.) (1987). *Readers, texts, teachers.* Portsmouth, NH: Heinemann Boynton/Cook.

Culler, J. (1983). *On deconstruction.* London: Routledge & Kegan Paul.

Fish, S. (1980). *Is there a text in this class? The authority of interpretive communities.* Cambridge, MA: Harvard University Press.

Iser, W. (1978). *The act of reading: A theory of aesthetic response.* Baltimore: The Johns Hopkins University Press.

Nelms, B. (Ed.). (1988). *Literature in the classroom: Readers, texts and contexts.* Urbana IL: NCTE.

Probst, R. (1988). Dialogue with a text. *English Journal,* 77(1), pp. 32–38.

Rosenblatt, L. (1978). *The reader, the text, the poem: The transactional theory of the literary work.* Carbondale: Southern Illinois University Press.

Scholes, R. (1982). *Semiotics and interpretation.* New Haven: Yale University Press.

Scholes, R. (1985). *Textual power: Literary theory and the teaching of English.* New Haven: Yale University Press.

It Gives You the Experience of What You Think

Gretchen Portwood Mathews
Robert Frost Intermediate School
Fairfax, Virginia

My students were enthusiastic readers, but I was troubled by their choices—at best, light fiction, bestsellers, and fantasy novels. *Sweet Valley High* and *Conan* type paperbacks also appeared occasionally from their hiding places in math books. My concern was how to get them to read more thoughtful novels without destroying their enthusiasm. At that time I taught literature via the traditional approach, where students answered the questions at the end of the story—a task most of them accomplished with competence and ease—without any real thought about what they were doing. After answering questions, the class would participate in the "whole class post-mortem" (Atwell, 1984). Because I believed the teacher held the responsibility for the success or failure of the operation, I worked hard—thinking, evaluating, organizing, synthesizing—to ensure that learning would take place. In the process, I learned a lot myself. It was an investment. I liked it. The lesson was my creation, my responsibility. I had bought into it and it mattered; it was mine. Sometimes I got rave reviews; at other times I was one of the few who learned anything.

I determined to try another method, this one involving self-directed reader responses to literature. The approach was appealing but frightening because the teacher had to give up control; it was also challenging because the process laid the responsibility for analysis in the students' hands. They would lead and I would follow. I first read about reader-response logs in an article by Orlean Anderson (1983).

Instead of responding to text questions, students write a journal entry giving an honest appraisal of what they read, questioning things they don't understand and reflecting on things they like and dislike. Anderson's article listed many prompts to pique students' imaginations, such as a reaction to a scene that triggered memories, or a discussion of a quote that a student found intriguing. Considered together, the prompts were a comprehensive look at a work of literature, but I worried that since a student would elect only a few, he or she might miss something important. The article noted, however, that invariably students brought out all the important concepts during discussion, which would consist of students reading their responses and other students responding. Concurrently, another colleague, Paul Russell, was taking a literature instruction class involving reader-response writing, and he shared his handout containing 37 additional ideas for responses. The possibilities seemed overwhelming, and not having every twist of the learning process planned ahead, including the answers, made me feel as though I would be reliving my first day of student teaching.

I was also beginning a new assignment: 140 eighth-graders. I hadn't taught eighth-graders in 12 years. I selected first a short story called "Marigolds" (Collier, 1969). It is a thoughtful, somewhat complex tale of Lizbeth, an adolescent black girl during the Depression, who faces what the author labels "a loss of innocence." Because Lizbeth's father is unemployed, her mother must work, and Lizbeth cares for her younger brother and entertains herself all day. Though older than most of the neighborhood children, she plays their games out of boredom, the favorite being to terrorize an old, eccentric woman named Miss Lottie. One night Lizbeth overhears her father sobbing about his unemployment, their poverty, and his doubts about his role as a provider. Her mother is comforting him. With her world turned upside down, Lizbeth rushes out to vent her frustrations on the only beautiful thing in her ugly existence, Miss Lottie's carefully tended marigolds. But before she can run away after her vandalism, Miss Lottie catches her. Lizbeth looks into her eyes and

> gazed upon a kind of reality which is hidden to childhood . . . [and knew] the end of innocence. . . . Innocence involves an unseeing acceptance of things at face value, an ignorance of the area below the surface. In that humiliating moment I looked beyond myself and into the depths of another person. This was the beginning of compassion, and one cannot have both compassion and innocence. (Collier, 1969, p. 545)

Since the story is loaded with perceptive comments on the nature of adolescence and growing up, I judged it to be perfect for us. Armed with a transparency of these quotes, I proceeded, confident that I would make connections. The girls liked the story; the boys hated it. The important "innocence" quote was beyond all of the boys and some of the girls:

> PATRICIA: I don't really understand the innocence she talks about, so this (her own experience similar to the character's) may not be a comparison, but I think it is, so here I go. . . . (It was.)
>
> KIM: . . . We live our life in boxes and you can't get in another box to gain something without losing something you had before. . . .
>
> JO: . . . I know it could really happen . . . a lot of other kids could relate to Lizbeth . . .
>
> JAY: You don't grow up in one day . . .
>
> JOHN: This is not the style of writing that I like.
>
> MARIE: There is a difference between ignoring others and innocence. Not everyone is a compassionate person. Some people don't think about others at all, but that is conceit and self-centeredness, not innocence.

Most adamant about his dislike of the story was Bryan. He hated these stories that teachers always picked out about relationships, and "Who cares about a bunch of marigolds?" Truly disconcerting was the degree of insight he demonstrated in his response; he *had* thought about it.

The next selection was "The Ransom of Red Chief" (Henry, 1907). Most passed this one off as "too light" or "too silly, this could never happen." Lisa wrote, "I got to thinking there had to be more to this story than I thought. After all, we were reading this in *English*, weren't we? I kept asking myself if I had read the right story." After that I selected "Indian Swing" (Rose, 1948), about a young boy whose family life is dull until another family with a philosophy about having fun together changes his perspective. He later discovers that the father has only a few months to live. Most said they knew right away that the father was going to die and that this made it worthless to read. I began to wonder just what they would appreciate and if I might be destroying their enthusiasm for reading.

When I presented the fourth story, Bryan, among others, asked, "Is this another story about relationships?" Smugly, I answered that it was an adventure story. He looked doubtful. "The Most Dangerous Game" (Connell, 1924) met with the most audience approval so far, though

Max said, "It has already been done on *Fantasy Island*" and Connie, summing up for many of the girls, called it "a sequel to *Rambo*."

I saved the best for last: "The Scarlet Ibis" (Hurst, 1960). The story, about a young boy's (the narrator) misguided sense of pride causing the death of his gentle, handicapped brother (Doodle), seemed to touch them.

JONAS: The sheer determination of the little boy to become somebody with the help of his brother was very moving.

MIKE: Doodle was a cool dude.

SELENE: Doodle seems like a saint or Christ. . . . He had such grace.

JESSICA: . . . We must accept people for who they are.

MONTI: . . . So realistic that it brought tears to my eyes. I hope that this was not a true story.

JOHN: It was interesting that the narrator sometimes had mixed feelings about his little brother. . . . These episodes made the story believable because unfortunately we all experience times when we feel mean or are tempted to do mean things, even to those we care about. Most of the time we resist the temptation and feel better about ourselves when we do.

SAM: It made me want to keep reading it, and not go away. That, to me, is always a sign of a good story.

These responses elicited rich contributions from other class members, but the one that truly brought the idea of universality to the students' awareness was Steven's response. During the discussion I had been aware of his indecision about raising his hand. Finally, he chose to share:

In "Scarlet Ibis" I could see all the workings of a great short story. I enjoyed it because it was poignant and definitely made me care. Doodle was expertly introduced to the story and almost immediately made the reader feel sorry for both Doodle and the narrator. I think that the idea of showing the point of view of a sibling of a child suffering from a birth defect is an excellent idea. I know this position for I was two when my sister was born. She suffered a few minor strokes as a two year old. This left her life permanently scarred with severe learning disabilities, aphasia, and extreme speech defects. I just disbelieved it at first. Then I tryed to help. Later in life I just could not understand it. I am in the gifted program and therefore a mental genius, yet here was my own sister who couldn't even be classified because she couldn't take a standard IQ test. When I was in third grade my parents fought viciously with the school system to attempt to get a specific label put on my sister. This story greatly reminded me of my own experience and I could easily see myself in the narrator's role, facing the same situations as he did.

Other class members listened intently to his reading. They realized that the story had further meaning: An experience very like it had happened to one of their friends. I thought we had taken a first giant step in understanding each other, as well as the story. They appeared to like writing reader responses, as if it were the first time they had been allowed to speak their minds, to let their own appraisals and avenues of investigation be heard. I surveyed my students about response writing; they definitely approved of the process:

- . . . a lot of work, but they help me understand the story.
- I let myself know how I feel about a story. I mean it's there in the back of my mind but when I write it, I understand it. Sounds crazy, huh?
- It makes you think more.
- It gives you the experience of what you think.
- You don't feel so limited.

Many responded that it allowed them to think about things other than plot. This revelation was particularly interesting since the only stipulation I had placed on the responses was "no plot summary"; apparently, they'd had enough of plot even though they had at first complained about this restriction. I asked them if they would prefer a more directed writing.

- No, then your thoughts might be wrong.
- Sometimes assignments are too specific, and I choke.
- I can choose what's best for me.
- It might be better for the teacher.

A majority revealed that they liked to read for fun, without thinking about an "English assignment," and for an initial "gut reaction." And most liked the idea of sharing their responses:

- An audience provides incentive.
- I like to explain things.
- You learn from others.

At this point, I read "Writing and Reading Literature from the Inside Out" (Atwell, 1984). The article describes her successful efforts to create "a literate environment . . . a place where people read, write, and talk about reading and writing, where everybody can be student and teacher, where everybody can come inside." I knew immediately that I liked Atwell's thinking, and it was also clear from the start that she had a rapport with her kids that fostered trust and acceptance, the first step in establishing a literate environment. It reminded me of an Emerson quote: "The secret of education lies in respecting the pupil" (Canfield and Wells, 1976, p. 38). Her thoughts closely paralleled my own because the article chronicled the conjunctive improvement of writing skills with the growth of literature appreciation. It inspired me to work harder to bring out my own kids' inner voices, those they had shown when responding to "The Scarlet Ibis" and to Steven's revelation. I wanted to build on that occurrence, for I believed it pointed to a way that would lead them to reading more thoughtful books. I defined *inner voice* as that which would give meaning or would encourage a kid to "come inside" (Atwell, 1984) a story or a novel. Renee had told me that learning happened when teachers understood the important difference between "encouragement and expectations." I surmised that teacher-selected stories symbolized expectations and that I had offered only a little encouragement for readers to depart from these expectations. I began to wonder what would happen if I removed them or at least disguised them, and added the extra encouragement of letting students select the literature.

Luck found me in the way of Stephen King. Many friends (students, teachers, others) had raved about the just-released movie *Stand by Me*, based on "The Body" (King, 1982). I was doubtful; the only King novel I had read was *Pet Sematary*, a book I'd wanted to toss into the Potomac. He'd gotten me involved with his characters; I cared about what happened to them, and then he copped out by using the supernatural to solve their problems. It was about as bad, I thought, as those student-woven plots of intrigue and complex characterization that got into such a spot that they had to be unraveled by having the narrator wake up from a dream. But, because of my respect for the people who recommended it (and with hesitancy about its R rating), I gave a bonus assignment: See *Stand by Me* with your parents and write a response. The responses showed the insights I'd hoped for from the short stories:

> JESSICA: You want to jump into the movie and experience. . . . You don't know exactly whether to laugh or to cry. It also brings you back to the time that either you or your parents experienced and gives you an understanding of how people were or are. . . .

VICKI: At the beginning my reaction was, "Oh, boy, this is going to be really funny!" But as it progressed, my feelings changed from happy to sad. Because of my emotion change, I thought about the film a little more. In that regard, my feeling at the end pertained mostly to my feelings throughout my life.

VIVIAN: They (the boys) showed compassion for the dead boy, which is kind of surprising from them. Usually they are the type that cause the problems . . . not the kind that cry and show they have feelings under their "tough kids" exterior.

SELENE: What a film! This movie will do all of us some good.

MATTHEW: "Marigolds" and it were alike in the way that the main characters were both torn between acting immature like everyone else or acting in a mature, cool way . . . both hit pretty much on the same theme, growing up.

CHARLIE: Five stars! The best drama I've ever seen.

DAVE: Most movies about children don't have children acting like children that age would really act. . . . The characters in *Stand By Me* are very realistic. Vern, who was supposed to be a wimp, was the only person that did not cry.

JACK: A mix of all the adolescent boys that ever existed, the story metaphors any struggle and would have special meaning to anyone who is experiencing or remembers the turmoil of adolescence.

ALICE: I wondered what had brought us here, and what would happen when we went home. Would our lives be the same? As the narrator says, "I never had friends like I had when I was twelve, but nobody does."

ANDREW: The kind of movie that got you thinking about things you don't really think of, like life and death and the meaning of it all. This story was one which makes me want to write a book and make a movie on my experiences as a child also to share with the world.

JONAS: The boys begin to act like adults: conservative, defensive, logical, cautious. . . .

Reading these reviews, I knew what I had hoped to be possible was indeed true: these kids could understand and write about everyman, about the universal aspects of being human. How could I build on this? Where could I fit in some classics? My first step was to view the movie. I saw what they saw: the ageless representation of growing up in all its glory and its misery. I was those kids; my kids were those kids. Stephen King had taught me something.

Anxious to discover the *why* and *how* of the experience, I decided to read the book. It was sold out everywhere, so I asked the kids if I might borrow someone's copy. The next morning, 30 minutes before school started, Eddie stood outside my door. Eddie was the most hyperactive of the nonsitters in my classes; he had an attention span of just over five minutes. In his hand was a copy of "The Body," with the beginning page marked, "since, Ms. Mathews, you see, this is an anthology. It's only one of the good books in here. I hope you like it." Eddie's morning visit marked the turning point, for it was the first time I really understood what Atwell's "literate environment" meant: trusting each other's judgment about literature. I hoped this was the initial step toward an appreciation of each other as readers. In Chapter 1 of "The Body," King writes:

> The most important things are the hardest things to say. They are the things you get ashamed of, because words diminish them—words shrink things that seemed limitless when they were in your head to no more than living size when they're brought out. But it's more than that, isn't it? The most important things lie close to wherever your secret heart is buried, like landmarks to a treasure your enemies would love to steal away. And you may make revelations that cost you dearly only to have people look at you in a funny way, not understanding what you've said at all, or why you thought it was so important that you almost cried while you were saying it. That's the worst, I think. When the secret stays locked within not for want of a teller but for want of an understanding ear. (King, 1982, p. 289)

The "understanding ear" seemed to fit naturally with the reader-response approach to literature, to be the key to unlocking the mystery of the inner voice, and to opening the door to an appreciation of literature. Concurrently, we were revising our monologue writings in reading-writing groups. I noticed the same sensitivity at work here, too, in the kids' own writing. It crossed all channels, from the content of the papers to the behaviors of the students as editors, to my own procedure during conferences with students. There was an aura of acceptance, a sense that this was indeed a safe place to reveal personal insights. Jacob, one of the outcasts, wrote a short story about his Halloween adventures with a lonely, punkish girl. It was expertly composed and showed much insight on the problems of adolescence. When reading-writing groups were formed, nobody had wanted Jacob in his or her group because of his carelessness with assignments and his tendency to goof off. After his group heard and commented on his paper, they all came to me to say how good his writing was.

Bryan, who had protested most loudly about our reading material, wrote "A Midsummer's Nightmare" about two diving coaches he'd known as a six-year-old. It was an interior monologue account of Patty and Ron. Patty had tortured him by seeing how tired and scared she could get him. Bryan wrote, "After a while, I just stopped doing anything for her. Then there was Ron." Ron "was fun, and honest, which is what I appreciated most. . . . I had done a belly flop, the best ever. Ron brought me to the ladder . . . and I climbed out, people clapped. I felt great. I went back and did another dive. This time Ron just watched. I was a professional, and I could dive like everyone else. Ron, he's [now] probably a senator or something, or teaching six-year-old kids how to swim."

Bryan's story was a metaphor for the understanding ear, though he didn't realize it. This listening channel was also evident in students' evaluations of the reading-writing groups and teacher conferences:

·   All the steps toward the manuscript helped, especially the revision group.

·   Everyone had a chance to speak his mind.

·   I knew my paper needed something, but I wasn't sure and the group helped me.

·   Students have so much to share with each other and groups are good sources of that togetherness that helps students share their thoughts.

·   I learned that writing takes more than a pen and a stack of paper; it takes planning, lots of editing, and hard work.

·   Groups are good for shy people—helps them open up and express their creativity.

·   Peers' comments weren't candy-coated or malicious; I did end up writing many drafts, but that's to be expected.

·   It was embarrassing to read out loud, but my paper wouldn't have been half as good.

·   It's easier to express yourself to people your own age.

·   There was no high-tech talk to confuse the student.

The comments about teacher conferences reflected something I hadn't realized that the kids thought important: They wanted me to like their writings as a reader. I found this particularly noteworthy because the survey was done after they had received their grades. The monologue manuscripts provided hours of pleasure reading for me, and I noted a peculiar attribute of nearly all of it: an awareness of writer's voice and audience. Previously, I had found it difficult to define, let alone teach, the concept of voice in writing. Though impossible to document, I believe this unexpected accomplishment directly correlated with students' having the opportunity to let their own voices speak in other areas of study: reading choices, reader responses, reading-writing groups, and teacher conferences.

I was still troubled, however, by the immaturity of their outside reading selections. Though only a few had ventured into what one student described as "the netherworld of classics," I noted that they *were* reading books recommended by their peers. I designed the next assignment to provide future models, to carry the inner voice and understanding ear a step further, to the point where students would select their outside reading choice from posters designed by their peers describing "Award-Winning Books."

At first, students were confused. "How do I know if it won an award? Can books win awards other than the Newbery?" So they did learn some adjunct lessons (e.g. there are reference books other than the encyclopedia); and they listened to their parents' recommendations as well as my own. In the process of researching, they also discovered the terms *Pulitzer, Nobel*, and *Edgar*. I learned a lot about science fiction, also Nebulas, Newberies, and the excellent work of adolescent fiction writers such as Irene Hunt, Cynthia Voit, and Katherine Paterson. The project had created a far-reaching network of librarians, books, kids, teachers, parents—Atwell's "literate environment." The novels selected ranged from *Charlotte's Web* to *Pride and Prejudice* to *Jacob Have I Loved* to *The Hunt for Red October*. I was pleased; we were approaching the consideration of noteworthy fiction chosen by students.

On the due day for the posters, students arrived very early to secure a prime spot for their masterpieces. They unveiled them from their plastic garbage bags, and I gave my praise to each. As I read their responses, I noted not only an analysis of plot, characters, and theme, but also an awareness of what Atwell calls "reading like writers and writing like readers." Students were looking into the craft of writing as well as searching for meaning. They were creative readers:

> Connie about *Huckleberry Finn*: The beginning reads: "Persons attempting to find a motive in this narrative will be prosecuted. Persons attempting to find a moral in this narrative will be banished. People attempting to find a plot in this narrative will be shot." This is the part of the book that got me interested in reading it.

Bill about *Taran*: I think this story is as good as it is because Lloyd Alexander adds a touch of realism to the story. Taran wants to be a hero, to feel important. This is a feeling most of us have when we are young. Unlike most of us, Taran gets his chance.

Jay about *Let the Circle Be Unbroken*: I kept wishing I could jump inside the book and help fight prejudice myself.

Bart about *Catcher in the Rye*: It had great action, not like *Rambo*, but mental action.

Ellen about *Jane Eyre*: I thoroughly enjoyed it despite the fact that my brothers said it was sappy. Which it wasn't because they hadn't even read it.

David about *The Chocolate War*: The author feels that teenagers are not very nice to each other.

Charlie about *Macbeth*: I wish someone would sit down and write Macbeth over again, using the language of today.

Andrew about *Rascal*: I always like books with a sad ending, even though I hate reading the sad ending. I can't handle sad endings because I really get into the book. [The beginnings of an appreciation of tragedy and perhaps even an elementary understanding of catharsis?]

Melissa about *The Grapes of Wrath*: Usually I'm afraid of Steinbeck's books, because they're so deep, but this was really good. When I first saw the title I thought it would be about a vineyard and a family's problems with it, like *Falconcrest*, but I was pleasantly surprised.

Jocelyn about *Great Expectations*: It would be easy to read if you were a dictionary. Even though the book was hard to read, the story was very, very, very, very clever. It would be worthless, not to mention idiotic, to suggest a better writing style to an author who's considered a great author . . . but if the author were just a no one writing a book, I'd probably suggest they use more common words that are easier to understand.

Timothy about *1984*: I think that after thinking about it, I guess the pros outweigh the cons, and therefore, it must be a good book.

The last student quote reflects many responses that started out in a somewhat negative vein and then proceeded to find some worth in the novel. It showed students writing to learn, finding meaning, and figuring out things via their inner voices.

We were then ready to begin *To Kill a Mockingbird* (Lee, 1960). Based on previous requests, I established "literate environment" days where class time was allowed for reading, writing, and private discussions about the book before we began our class discussion. On the first day scheduled for discussion, I was nervous. Though I had observed that they appeared to like the novel, I had really exposed my own inner voice about my favorite novel, hoping for an encouraging ear. I began by asking, "What's your gut reaction?" They loved it—even Bryan, who had hated "Marigolds" so much. Even more important, he felt comfortable about saying so, perhaps even gushing a bit, in front of the entire class. They spoke of Atticus' courage, of the injustice dealt Tom Robinson, and how Scout and Jem were just like them when they were kids. The realists explained to the idealists why Tom Robinson gave up and tried to escape.

In all classes, our discussion was the most stimulating I've experienced in 16 years of teaching, including a year's stint in Advanced Placement. They didn't need me, but allowed me to participate. Dean wondered what Scout meant when she said Jem looked like he'd been crying but she hadn't heard him. This incident occurs after Jem realizes that Nathan Radley cemented the knot hole to keep Boo from carrying out his vicarious friendship with Scout and Jem. Jo explained to Chang that people don't cry out loud anymore as they get older. And then Ben asked why Jem was crying. The hands flew into the air, but Bryan's was the most insistent. He spoke, "It's like in that marigolds story . . . you know . . . the innocence thing, how you don't realize things. Like when, what . . . what's her name . . ."

Another student chimed in, "Lizbeth."

"When Lizbeth realizes how mean she'd been to that old lady, when she felt sorry for her. It's the same with Jem; he sees that Boo just wants to be friends. Especially since Boo sewed up his pants and didn't tell Atticus about them prowling around that night. Jem sees that Boo isn't an awful creep like he used to think. That's why he cries, because he's feeling sorry for Boo." Bryan looked pretty pleased with himself, and I was speechless. The rest of the class were nodding in agreement. I hadn't made that connection, but the kids immediately saw it. It was evaluation, Bloom's highest level of thinking.

The culminating assignment for *To Kill a Mockingbird* was a paper based on their responses. Excerpts from these papers demonstrate students' awareness of and confidence in expressing their own inner voices as they interacted with the novel. They evaluated the novel, "reading like writers and writing like readers" (Atwell, 1984):

JONATHAN: When you read the book you feel that Atticus is fair but brave, courageous, a good parent and full of other attributes. When I thought about this, I came to the conclusion that this was how Harper Lee wanted you to perceive Atticus, and she succeeded.

AMY: Atticus was, in the words of Shakespeare, "a proper man, as one shall see in a summer's day; a most lovely, gentleman-like man."

JON: Webster's definition of courage is "a lack of fear." Atticus's definition ["It's when you know you're licked before you begin but you begin anyway and you see it through no matter what. You rarely win but sometimes you do." (Lee, 1960)] is much better. If you had to fight someone, there would be no fear if you had a definite advantage. Such a person is not courageous because he knows he is going to win.

MARK: Atticus Finch is one of the most admirable characters I have come to know through all of my readings.

Last week we did our most recent book writing. I had prepared a list of prompts for responding, such as recommending the protagonist to an Ivy League college, interviewing the protagonist on a television talk show, or writing the protagonist's eulogy. I noticed many of the kids chewing their pen caps and gazing into the courtyard. "What's the matter," I asked.

Melancholic Mark, who had just recently tackled Dostoevsky's *Notes from Underground* after I had mentioned the darkness of Russian novels, looked up and said, somewhat condescendingly. "These questions don't cover what I have to say. They're kind of silly, really, when you think about my book." I noted nods of agreement, encouraging ears. So I followed suit and asked, "What would you rather do?"

"Can't we write our own reactions and feelings? I have a lot to say about this book."

"Of course," I answered. "I'm glad you do."

REFERENCES

Anderson, O. (1983). Teaching literature through reader response. *Handbook for teaching the gifted*. Fairfax, VA: Fairfax County Public Schools.

Atwell, N. (1984). Writing and reading literature from the inside out. *Language Arts, 61.* (3), pp 240–252.

Canfield, J. & Wells, H.C. (1976). *100 ways to enhance self-concept in the classroom.* Englewood Cliffs, NJ: Prentice-Hall.

Collier, E. (1969). Marigolds. In G. R. Carlsen & R.C. Carlsen (Eds.), *Perception* (pp. 538–545). New York: McGraw-Hill.

Connell, R. (1924). The most dangerous game. In E.J. Gordon (Ed.), *The study of literature* (pp. 5–25). Boston: Ginn.

Henry, O. (1907). The ransom of red chief. In E.J. Gordon (Ed.), *The study of literature* (pp. 58–67). Boston: Ginn.

Hurst, J. (1960). The scarlet ibis. In R. C. Pooley, J. Stuart, L. White, J. Cline, and O.S. Niles (Eds.), *Outlooks through literature* (pp. 87–95). Chicago: Scott, Foresman.

King, S. (1982). The body. *Different seasons.* New York: New American Library, pp. 289–433.

Lee, H. (1960). *To kill a mockingbird.* New York: Fawcett.

Rose, R. (1948). Indian swing. In G.R. Carlsen & R.C. Carlsen (Eds.), *Perception* (pp. 566–576). New York: McGraw-Hill.

Hearing Yourself Think: Responding to Text through Monologue

Gillian Clarkson

Write to Learn Project, Wiltshire, England

*I*n the past 20 years, group talk has become part of the learning repertoire, with the growing understanding that it is through talk that we all make sense of the world around us, discovering vital connections between what we already know and understand and the new ideas and experiences that confront us. Rather than feeding pupils with gobbets of information to be swallowed whole, teachers are creating opportunities for their students to talk together to chew over and digest new concepts and new knowledge, the better to understand and so learn.

Talking together with a small group of trusted peers enables students to test ideas; sharing their existing knowledge and their past experience helps them interpret the new. Different viewpoints suggest different interpretations, so that the study of a text becomes a joint exploration to discover layers of meaning beyond what was immediately apparent; and the need to explain to others what was only tentatively grasped helps students clarify and extend these emerging perceptions. But group talk is hard work and has its own pressures and constraints that inhibit some students. Not everyone is confident enough to take an active part in such sharing of half-formed ideas, and the quick bouncing around of several ideas makes it difficult for any single concept to be fully explored. However patient other members of the group may be, no one speaker can have unlimited time to grope toward a new awareness or to continue to redraft his or her expression to clarify its meaning.

For some students, on some occasions, the opportunity to record a taped monologue may provide a freedom to extend and explore that group talk prohibits. Talking to an unresponsive machine has its own problems, but there is time to think. Moreover, a student working in this way can play back what has already been said and, hearing his or her own thoughts, can develop and amend them without interruption. I should like to offer two examples of taped monologues for you to consider, from students of very different levels of ability. In both, the students reach levels of understanding that would, I think, be unlikely either in the bustle of group discussion or in writing.

The first monologue was taped by a tenth-grade student, a "school failure" for whom writing is so difficult that thinking with the written word is almost impossible. So much effort is required to find and shape each letter and struggle with spelling that there is little energy left for thinking. Before Michael recorded his thoughts, his teacher had read the opening section of Steinbeck's *Of Mice and Men*—up to George and Lennie's arrival at the ranch—to the whole class. The students were asked to talk together, in small friendship groups, about what they had learned of the two main characters. As was usual, Michael played no active part in this discussion. He had become used to the idea of his own lack of ability and believed he could have nothing to contribute.

When the students were asked to write about their understanding of George and Lennie, the teacher suggested that Michael might like to try and put his words on tape, although he had never done so before. He was shown how to use the pause button, so that he could stop and think whenever he wished, and it was suggested that, if he got stuck, he could play back what he had already said to remind himself of his own thoughts and perhaps see how he might continue. Michael stayed on his own with the text and the tape for the remainder of the lesson, emerging some 20 minutes later with the tape and the comment that "It was ok!" The reasons for his teacher's more enthusiastic response to the recorded monologue can best be seen in the following transcript of

Michael's thoughts. (Throughout the transcripts, + indicates a use of the pause button; / indicates the phrasing.)

I think Lennie is a good guy to George / no George is
a good guy to Lennie / but there's only one problem / er /
Lennie always keeps forgetting / what to do / and all that
lot / but / George is like a brother to Lennie / George
5 helps him what to say / and what to do and / George stays
with Lennie because +
      No / George stays with Lennie because Lennie is a
good worker / and if he works before he talks / he
probably gets the job / but if he talks before he works /
10 they won't get a job / George needs Lennie / to do all the
things like that / but +
      George keeps Lennie out of trouble / wherever he /
wherever George and Lennie goes / Lennie always gets into
trouble / like feeling girls' dresses / I think he likes
15 feeling soft things +
      Lennie likes having soft things / and +
      George is quite cruel to Lennie / er / George / but
George / gives / but George says sorry after he's said
things / like when he / when he chucked the mouse +
20   When he chucked the mouse away / he felt sorry for
him / and George / George / Lennie went and got it / and
George knew he went to it / and got it / but George had
to chuck it away / because / it was dead / but if Lennie
found a real one / George'd let him keep it +
25   George is looking after Lennie / 'cos if George left
Lennie / Lennie wouldn't get on very well / so George /
George is like a brother to him / or a father +
      Lennie believes in story-time / or fairy tales / like
that / but when he tells him about the rabbits / he makes
30 Lennie really / very happy / like Lennie is / er / seeing
all the time / er / heard it all the time / George /
George is very good to Lennie +
      If George never had Lennie / George / would be out of
a job / George wouldn't have no friends / Lennie wouldn't
35 have no friends / nor George / but Lennie helps him get /
most of the money / and they're buddies or pals +
      Lennie believes in fairy tales / because one day /
they might have something like a rabbit hutch / on a farm
/ like pigs in it / and all that lot +
40   George says to Lennie / [reads] "I wish I could put
you in a cage with about a million mice and let you have
fun," / then George feels sorry for Lennie / after he said
all that +
      Lennie argues with George / because when they was
45 having that can of beans / over the fire / George wanted

some ket . . . / Lennie wanted some ketchup / but George said
they never had none / George kept on arguing / he goes /
he goes / Lennie said to George / he goes / [reads] "I was
only fooling about George, I don't want no ketchup. I
50 wouldn't eat no ketchup if it was right here beside me."

The tape is interesting for a variety of reasons, not least for the way
Michael argues closely from the text, quoting to support his point; but
I should like to consider the way that Michael develops, through his
talk, his understanding of the relationship between the two men. He
tackles the subject immediately: "I think Lennie is a good guy to
George / no George is a good guy to Lennie," and "George is like a
brother to Lennie" (lines 1 and 4). He understands that there is a
relationship, that these are not just casual acquaintances who have
met on the road, because George takes care of Lennie as an older
brother might. Michael can see that the relationship is not totally one-
sided: "Lennie is a good worker" (line 8), and "George needs Lennie /
to do all the things like that" (line 10). The pause after the word *but*
which follows this statement seems to be because Michael realizes the
complexity of the friendship. George isn't simply exploiting Lennie as
a meal ticket, although that is perhaps Michael's first idea: "George
stays with Lennie because Lennie is a good worker" (line 7). Had he
continued to believe this, I think Michael would have used the word *so*
and continued the sentence: "George needs Lennie to do all the things
like that SO George keeps Lennie out of trouble." The word *but* (line
11) suggests that Michael has had second thoughts and chooses not to
pursue that line of argument.

After some consideration of Lennie's liking for soft things, Michael
states, "George is quite cruel to Lennie" (line 17). However, this
thought is immediately modified: "but George says sorry after he's
said things" (line 18), giving an example from the text to support his
contention. George is not unkind because he is a cruel man. He feels
sympathy for Lennie but realizes that he must be protected from the
danger a dead and rotting mouse might pose. This understanding
seems to enable Michael to clarify the earlier problem which he
appeared to have shelved at line 10. George does not stay with Lennie
only to profit from the latter's hard work but because, "if George left
Lennie / Lennie wouldn't get on very well / so George is like a brother
to him / or a father" (lines 25–27). The addition of *or a father* suggests
that Michael has understood that George feels a responsibility to—and
for—Lennie greater than that between siblings. He develops this idea
with the story telling, an example of the father–son relationship, and

once again stops the machine—to rethink that interdependence in the relationship that makes it different from that between parent and child.

When he begins again, after a mighty sigh, he has developed his understanding still further and is able to state what each offers the other: "If George never had Lennie / George / would be out of a job" (line 33) . . . "Lennie helps him get / most of the money" (line 35). However, they need one another's friendship equally: "George wouldn't have no friends / Lennie wouldn't have no friends" (line 34). The relationship is not that of brothers, or of father and son, although there are elements of both in their friendship. No, each needs the other; they are "buddies or pals" (line 36).

The difference between these relationships is not an easy concept to grasp, but Michael has been able to reach that understanding. What might at first glance seem a random and hesitant set of utterances, interspersed with examples from the text, is, in fact, a tightly woven development of a complex idea. His thinking is able to refine itself because each step, once uttered, suggests the next after a period of reflection. He is able to shape and reshape because he has had time to do so without interruption by or pressure from others.

The second monologue is from an eleventh-grade girl—a bright and articulate student, a confident and very competent writer—who had chosen English Literature as one of three subjects to be studied to advanced level in her last two years at school. The background to the recording was also different from that which produced Michael's monologue. I asked her to make the recording because I was interested to see how much we could capture on tape of an individual's thought processes, when faced with a new and difficult problem. Because I wanted to catch as much as possible of what normally would be an internal monologue, I asked Virginia to leave the tape recorder running, neither using the pause button nor playing back what she had already uttered. I gave her Sylvia Plath's "Blackberrying," a poem she hadn't read before; nor, as far as she remembered, had she read anything else by Plath. There was no chance for her to study the poem, nor to listen to or share anyone else's perceptions.

Virginia stayed with the poem and the tape recorder for nearly an hour, circling her way several times through the poem, deconstructing it and reconstructing it in the light of her own experience, asking herself questions and making new discoveries. It is difficult to choose any one part from such a long and complex recording, where thoughts are so closely interwoven, but it is clearly impossible to give it all. She begins by reading the poem:

Blackberrying

Nobody in the lane, and nothing, nothing but blackberries,
Blackberries on either side, though on the right mainly,
A blackberry alley, going down in hooks, and a sea
Somewhere at the end of it, heaving. Blackberries

5 Big as the ball of my thumb, and dumb as eyes
Ebon in the hedges, fat
With blue-red juices. These they squander on my fingers.
I had not asked for such a blood sisterhood; they must love me.
They accommodate themselves to my milkbottle, flattening their
    sides.

10 Overhead go the choughs in black, cacophonous flocks—
Bits of burnt paper wheeling in a blown sky.
Theirs is the only voice, protesting, protesting.
I do not think the sea will appear at all.
The high, green meadows are glowing, as if lit from within.

15 I come to one bush of berries so ripe it is a bush of flies,
Hanging their bluegreen bellies and their wing panes in a Chinese
    screen.
The honey-feast of berries has stunned them; they believe in heaven.
One more hook, and the berries and bushes end.

The only thing to come now is the sea.

20 From between two hills a sudden wind funnels at me,
Slapping its phantom laundry in my face.
These hills are too green and sweet to have tasted salt.
I follow the sheep path between them. A last hook brings me
To the hills' northern face, and the face is orange rock

25 That looks out on nothing, nothing but a great space
Of white and pewter lights, and a din like silversmiths
Beating and beating at an intractable metal.

Unsure how to begin, Virginia starts to consider one line at a time, sometimes at length, glossing over others until she reaches line 6:

. . . Anyway / and then she talks about / how the / she gets the
blood on her fingers / which I think's effective / because you do get
your hands / and it does look like blood / you feel as though /
you're killing them when you pick them / and it's really / a weird
idea about / "they must love me" / giving the blood of sisterhood /
and I don't understand what "my milkbottle" is / "they accommodate themselves to my milkbottle, flattening their sides / [pause] /
"to my milkbottle" / oh / she / she puts them / she puts them in a
milkbottle / she collects them in a milkbottle / . . .

As Virginia begins this first sortie into the poem, she seems to be
trying out for herself how much she can make sense of at once. Ideas
are jumbled together: the sensitive comment, "you feel as though
you're killing them as you pick them," tossed out as she tries to make
sense of the mundane milkbottle. It is obvious that a milkbottle has no
place in Virginia's experience of blackberrying, and she almost begins
to explore some metaphorical meaning. You can hear the excitement
on the tape in her tone of voice as she solves the problem. The eureka-
like "oh" is followed by a sudden increase in pace as the explanation is
discovered and given.

After going through the whole poem in sequence, she circles
through it again until she comes back to those lines:

. . . "blackberries big as the ball" / "juices" / well I mentioned that
before / [pause] / "These they squander on my fingers" / they /
they squander their blue-red juices / they / "I had not" / they / "I
had not asked for such a blood sisterhood; they must love me" / why
do you think it's "sisterhood"? / is it sisterhood because she's female?
/ blood / but / does that mean the black / blackberries / have to
be female too? / 'cos I'd never tried to put a personality to blackberries / I wonder if they're / essentially feminine / or masculine / it
would be interesting to look at their / um / articles in German,
French and Spanish / I think they're feminine in German / and I
can't remember what they are in French or Spanish / oh / because /
if you think of blackberries as / what they / they / they cover
everywhere / blackberries / brambles / when you think of
blackberries and brambles / they cover any / everywhere / they
sort of spread / and they scratch / and they stop people / they /
they're resistant / and blackberries themselves are / dark and
prolific / well / [pause] / that doesn't really get me anywhere / I
just thought that / sort of scratching was feminine / it had feminine
/ catty associations but / actual blackberries / I'm not really sure /
[pause] / anyway / it's strange that they squander blood sisterhood
/ because / because / um / you think of blood brothers etcetera /
as a religious and special sort of / um / rite / and that they
squander it seems very / haphazard and nonchalant and / careless
and wasteful . . .

Virginia may be right that this thoughtful passage, "doesn't really get me anywhere," and it is certain that these ideas would be unlikely to find their way into a "lit-crit" essay. Nevertheless, the fact that she continues to explore them beyond the point where she apparently dismisses them as useless, suggests that it was necessary for her to work through this confusion before she could move on. Those lines are part of the poem, and to ignore them or to gloss over them is to ignore part of the poem's experience. Perhaps, like Plath, Virginia is exploring what it is to be female: blood, they cover and spread and scratch, they stop people, they're resistant, dark and prolific, scratching, catty. And is our blood, the life in us, squandered in the "haphazard and nonchalant and careless and wasteful" way that Virginia suggests?

She creates and extends thoughts, making connections as she talks and new ideas as she utters them. From the broken sentence, sighs, and pauses, it sounds as though she is groping her way with no idea that each utterance "constitutes a stage on a purposeful journey" (Britton, 1982) toward an understanding of herself and, perhaps, of Plath. At a deeper level, she seems to sense the importance of this exploration for, despite her rejection of it as unhelpful, she comes back to it with "I just thought . . ." A growing idea, like a healthy fetus, is not readily aborted.

Throughout this long monologue, Virginia asks herself direct questions to help focus her attention; uses her existing knowledge (of other languages, for example, or later, of biology when she talks of the separate parts of the blackberry fruit being like "the compound eye of a fly"); translates the poem in terms of her own experience, talking of mountain walks when, like Plath, she notices fields "glowing, as if lit from within" (line 14). At every step she gives the poem a reality for herself by forging connections between the text and her own experience and knowledge.

It may be that, had I asked Virginia to write in a similar way—as a sort of stream of consciousness—she would have made similar connections, explored similar questions, but I think it unlikely. In some places in the recording, the words rush out in a sudden spate, too fast for writing to catch. At other times, the slowness, the inexactitude, the groping for thoughts still too shadowy to shape themselves even in the spoken word make it unlikely that she would have tried to write them at all. Like the shape at the edge of our vision that recedes as we try to focus on it, such vague notions would disappear before the greater exactness that writing demands. Recognizing their vagueness she would, as most of us do, try to rehearse them in her head before trying to catch them in writing. If they were not amenable to such shaping, she would no doubt have omitted them.

On the tape recorder, she tries to talk these ideas into existence, without prior rehearsal. They may remain sketchy and incomplete, but at least we can know something of these thoughts through the few broken phrases. At one point in the recording, for example, she tries to connect the repeated "nothing, nothing" of the first line with that in line 25: "That looks on nothing, nothing but a great space."

> It's not / [pause] / it's about / something different / it's about / it says / "and the face is an orange rock That looks out on nothing, nothing but a great space Of white and pewter lights" / and you have that "nothing, nothing" / which gives you an immediate / sort of / view / image / feeling of emptiness / . . .

The connection Virginia strives for is never made, although in the process of trying, others emerge. Had she not tried to pursue the initial idea, as I believe she would not have done in writing since she decides "it's about / something different," she might not have come to the notion of the "view / image / feeling of emptiness" to which she returns much later in the recording. Like Michael, Virginia has been able to extend her thinking because she had time to do so, and because the connections she strove to make were able to be given shape through her own words. However vague the first shape that emerges, words give it a reality more solid than that which exists, wordless in our heads. Once she has heard what she thought, then she can modify that thought.

In her introduction to *Mostly about Writing* (1983), Janet Emig writes of talk being focused "on the speaker's own vision" which "gives access to thinking." In these two examples, the speakers' visions—Michael's vision of what friendship between "buddies or pals" can be; Virginia's growing awareness of what it is to be female—not only give access to thinking but power the flow of words that creates the flow of thoughts. Because opportunity was given to focus on that vision and so unlock the words, connections were made and understandings reached that might not otherwise have been possible.

Any contexts that provide such opportunities for extended thinking deserve a place in our classrooms. Perhaps the monologue might, on some occasions, for some students, encourage them to explore and develop their own understandings of, and responses to, a text. You will certainly lose nothing by offering them the choice.

REFERENCES

Britton, J. (1982). Talking. In G. M. Pradl (Ed.), *Prospect and retrospect: Selected essays of James Britton*. Portsmouth, NH: Boynton/Cook.

Emig, J. (1983). Introduction. In N. Martin, *Mostly about writing*. Portsmouth, NH: Boynton/Cook.

Nonfiction Literature in the Writing Class

Tom Reigstad
Buffalo State College

*I*n recent years, reader-response theory has focused on what happens in the transaction between reader and text. This transaction has been described in various ways. Alan C. Purves and Victoria Rippere (1968) suggest that readers be held accountable for their reactions. For example, a reader making a summary statement about a literary work should be prepared to support it. For Louise Rosenblatt (1978), the text arouses associations, feelings, attitudes, and ideas that help guide what the text activates in the reader and what the reader activates in the text. David Bleich (1975) emphasizes how a reader projects desires on a text.

What these theories have in common is that they invite readers to engage themselves in highly active, personal ways with the texts they encounter. But Marjorie Roemer (1987) warns of two obstacles for putting reader-response theory into practice: the tendency of students to lapse into giving objective, traditional responses no matter how much they are encouraged to do otherwise; and the fact that teachers might repress students by not being truly committed to accepting "a plurality of readings" by students.

I'd like to describe a sequence of writing assignments which I designed with Roemer's cautions in mind. The writing tasks require my first-year college students to respond to major nonfiction works as literary and affective blueprints for them to react to in personal ways. I'll illustrate this approach with Twain's *The Innocents Abroad* (1980).

120

First, a bit of background on the book: At the age of 31, Twain was paid by a California newspaper, *The Alta California*, to join a tour group making a pilgrimage to the Holy Land by way of Europe. He sent back letters about his trip which the newspaper published and which eventually served as the basis for his book. Even though *The Innocents Abroad* was available only from door-to-door canvassers, it sold over 100,000 copies in its first three years (Dickinson, 1947). The book is regarded as America's first nonfiction best-seller.

In *The Innocents Abroad*, I found a mother lode of devices that Twain used to emphasize and enhance his comically satirical view of an American abroad. Twain relies on exaggeration, slapstick, and puns to poke fun at himself, his fellow travelers, and the places he visits. He is particularly adept at pacing his humorous passages. In an essay titled "How to Tell a Story," Twain (1962) describes the posture of a deadpan narrator using the verbal trick of telling an apparently rambling, disjointed story that closes with a twist, or what he calls "a nub, a point, or a snapper." One episode in *The Innocents Abroad*, when Twain visits the ruins of Pompeii, illustrates this technique (Twain, 1980):

> But perhaps the most poetical thing Pompeii has yielded to modern research was that grand figure of a Roman soldier clad in complete armor, who, true to his duty, true to his proud name of a soldier of Rome, and full of the stern courage which had given to that name its glory, stood to his post by the city gate, erect and unflinching, till the hell that raged around him *burned out* the dauntless spirit it could not conquer.
>
> We never read of Pompeii but we think of that soldier; we cannot write of Pompeii without the natural impulse to grant to him the mention he so well deserves. Let us remember that he was a soldier— not a policeman—and so praise him. Being a soldier, he stayed— because the warrior instinct forbade him to fly. Had he been a policeman, he would have stayed also—because he would have been asleep. (pp. 240–241)

My students study this passage: the slow serio-comic buildup, leading to the delivery of the punch line. Then we compare it to the tame, bland version Twain sent in as correspondent for *The Alta California* (Dickinson, 1947):

> In a stone sentry-box, just outside the city wall, we saw where the gallant mail-clad soldier stood his fearful watch that dreadful night, till he died, scorning to desert his post till he heard the relief call which was never more to sound. (p. 152)

This version, devoid of humor, helps students see the care Twain put into his revision of the scene for later publication. Students also discuss possible reasons for Twain's changes.

There are many examples of how Twain uses an effective "contrastive" strategy to describe some of the disappointing ventures on his journey. I tie in our study of how Twain uses contrast with a chapter from Ken Macrorie's *Telling Writing* (1985). Macrorie advises writers to "make it a habit to look for oppositions. You will find suddenly that you are wiser than you thought. Do it automatically. If you find yourself putting down *hot*, consider the possibility of *cold* in the same circumstances. . . . The result is tension" (pp. 71–74). Twain's encounter with the Parisian barber in *The Innocents Abroad* uses the "opposition" of expectation versus reality masterfully. Again the scene is deliberately set up, in order to heighten the irony of his high expectations (Twain, 1980):

> From earliest infancy it had been a cherished ambition of mine to be shaved some day in a palatial barbershop in Paris. I wished to recline at full length in a cushioned invalid chair, with pictures about me and sumptuous furniture; with frescoed walls and gilded arches above me and vistas of Corinthian columns stretching far above me; with perfumes of Araby to intoxicate my senses and the slumbrous drone of distant noises to soothe me to sleep. At the end of an hour I would wake up regretfully and find my face as smooth and as soft as an infant's. Departing, I would lift my hands above that barber's head and say, "Heaven bless you, my son!" . . . I said I wanted to be shaved. . . . Then there was an excitement among those two barbers! There was a wild consultation, and afterwards a hurrying to and fro and a feverish gathering up of razors from obscure places and a ransacking for soap. Next they took us into a little mean, shabby back room; they got two ordinary sitting-room chairs and placed us in them with our coats on. . . . I sat bolt upright, silent, sad, and solemn. One of the wig-making villains lathered my face for ten terrible minutes and finished by plastering a mass of suds into my mouth. . . . Then this outlaw strapped his razor on his boot, hovered over me ominously for six fearful seconds, and then swooped down upon me like the genius of destruction. The first rake of his razor loosened the very hide from my face and lifted me out of the chair. I stormed and raved. . . . (pp. 84–85)

About this time I ask students to think of an event that they have looked forward to—a concert, a dinner, a dance—and try their hand at a brief, three- to four-paragraph account patterned after a Twainian contrastive beginning. Here are openings by two students which plant clear contrastive clues:

Student #1:

When I was asked to go to the prom I was so happy. I ran out to find the perfect gown. Not just any gown would do. It took me a while, but I found the most beautiful dress in the whole world. My date wore a tux that matched me to a tee. My spirits were so high when I walked out of my front door, but they were soon to be let down lower than low. As I was walking down the steps of my porch, my date stepped on the back of my gown. I kept walking, but my gown didn't. . . .

Student #2:

All through high school I dreamt about going down to Florida during Christmas vacation. I could just see the beaches now. The sun would be shining. It would be hot, but not warm enough to sweat in. I would lounge on the beach all day not doing anything more than lifting the tropical drink to my mouth. Of course, everywhere you looked there would be beautiful women. Every hour or so some beautiful women would offer to rub my back with suntan lotion. This would be a great week of rest and relaxation. . . .

In addition to written exercises like these, where students attempt some of Twain's stylistic gimmicks, they also write in text-based ways. They produce a research paper on *The Innocents Abroad* and an in-class essay exam. I devise essay questions that ask students to analyze *The Innocents Abroad* by using some of the categories of writing style suggested by William Zinsser in *On Writing Well* (1985), another text for the course. They are invited to write positive or negative reviews of *The Innocents Abroad* as in these examples:

Question #1:

In 1869 a leading magazine, *Packard's Monthly*, published a favorable review of *Innocents Abroad*, citing Mark Twain's humor. If you, too, were impressed with the humor in *Innocents Abroad*, compose your own piece of criticism. Incorporate Zinsser's suggestions, using "as much specific detail as possible" by "allowing the author's words to do their own documentation." (Zinsser, 1985, p. 84)

Question #2:

Several published reactions to *Innocents Abroad* in 1869 were less than complimentary. Twain was pictured as an ignorant, raucous frontiersman romping through venerable lands, sneering and laughing at everything foreign. A British critic found the book "offensive, . . . supremely contemptuous, . . . ostentatiously and atrociously vulgar," while the *New York Tribune* deplored its "offensive irreverence." If you agree that *Innocents Abroad* is offensive, write a piece of negative criticism pointing to specific sources of your displeasure. Don't get too carried away with your own wit. Remember Zinsser's advice to be personable and opinionated. (Zinsser, 1985, p. 145)

Students generally fare quite well when picking one of these questions to respond to. Some even introduce their exams innovatively. One student started her exam this way:

> Have you ever been invited to a friend's house for dinner only to be bored with vacation stories or, worse yet, slides? The trip becomes even more foreign to you. Travel books can have the same alienating, deadening effect. The author should speak in a personal manner, creating a common ground, giving the reader something to relate to. It takes skill to write about travels, a secure personality to recognize and relay human flaws, and an excellent wit to put the two together. Mark Twain had this ability and used it well in his travel masterpiece, *Innocents Abroad.*

With a carefully planned sequence of activities that elicits written responses both connected to the text and using it as a point of departure, students seem to benefit more from their reading. But with writing assignments integrated with their study of a best-selling travel book, students become better readers and better writers.

In end-of-semester evaluations, students gave high marks to *The Innocents Abroad.* One student wrote: "Although I'm sure that things have changed where Twain once traveled, the experiences seen through his eyes will always be informative and funny to new readers." For a generation of television "couch potatoes," what better endorsement could there be of the power of reading for inexperienced writers?

REFERENCES

Bleich, D. (1975). *Readings and feelings.* Urbana, IL: National Council of Teachers of English.

Dickinson, L. (1947). Mark Twain's revisions in writing *The Innocents Abroad. American Literature, 19,* pp. 139–157.

Macrorie, K. (1985). *Telling writing.* Portsmouth, NH: Boynton/Cook.

Purves, A., & Rippere, V. (1968). *The elements of writing about a literary work.* Urbana, IL: National Council of Teachers of English.

Roemer, M. (1987). Which reader's response? *College English, 49,* pp. 911–921.

Rosenblatt, L. M. (1978). *The reader, the text, the poem.* Carbondale: Southern Illinois University Press.

Twain, M. (1962). How to tell a story. In W. Blair (Ed.), *Selected shorter writings of Mark Twain* (pp. 239–243). Boston: Houghton Mifflin.

Twain, M. (1980). *The innocents abroad.* New York: Signet. Reprint.

Zinsser, W. (1985). *On writing well.* New York: Harper & Row.

Retelling

Teachers often try to wrestle their students into an understanding of "literary techniques"—plot, character, symbol, figurative language. I have constructed elaborate and gimmicky lessons to help students understand ("be able to identify") allegory, parable, dramatic irony, iambic pentameter, and on and on and onomatopoeia. I am uncomfortable with this approach to teaching literature because it is reductive, based on one narrow critical theory, and treats books like chocolate cakes: Readers will be more appreciative if they know the ingredients.

—*Candida Gillis*

Storytelling—In High School? Honestly.

Marni Schwartz

Niskayuna Middle School,
Schenectady, New York

As I write this, the movie *Cry Freedom* (Attenborough, 1987) is still singing in my bones. I'm glad I have it on tape so I can see it again and again. Soon, while its music and images still croon in the marrow. But later too, years from now, when retrospect will allow me to see how it touched my work as a storyteller and the work of others angered and frightened by its honesty.

I have been coming to an understanding of how storytelling is another road, another method of travel, really, down the road toward maturing literacy. Seeing *Cry Freedom* reinforced this notion. Its brutal images, its repetition of Stephen Biko's words, and its intermingled sounds of African music and gunfire will continue to haunt me just as do the powerful images and sounds of tales told to me aloud. I recommend storytelling as one more way to help adolescents into literature, into their own writing, and into the self and social awareness we hope they will take from high school into the world.

Ellen Rosenblum, age 16, co-presented with me this year at a local conference. She first told stories "a long time ago" in my middle school classroom at age 11 and has continued to do so through her camp job, her Hebrew studies, various shows, and competitions she's entered on her own. We've stayed in touch, a little, so I thought of her for the presentation. I hoped a student's words about storytelling would add credence to mine. As we prepared for the session, she said she wanted to talk about how storytelling offered her the chance to be different people or things. "I just loved practicing the mean voice of Elizabeth," she said about the antagonist in *Molly's Pilgrim* (Cohen, 1983). During the session, Ellen recalled for us some of the roles storytelling had offered her in the past from "being Christmas" in Sendak's *Chicken Soup with Rice* (1962) to singing as a foolish frog puffing up with pride till he exploded (P. Seeger & C. Seeger, 1973), a role for which she won first prize in a large competition. After Ellen's telling of the story of Molly, who discovers that her mother's understanding of "pilgrim" doesn't match the image her classmates hold, a teacher asked Ellen why she had chosen *Molly's Pilgrim* for the conference.

> When I tell it to little kids it shows them it's not always good to tease, and a lot of times they pick on other kids. I guess adults might not need it that way, but I think it says a lot about racism too. How, you know, not all Russians are peasants but I guess that's the way a lot of people think about it. It's kind of a stereotypical thing that you can eliminate by telling a story like this. And, um, I just *really* like this story. It's just really great telling a story and being different, being a different person 'cause sometimes you just have to get away from who you are.

Telling stories helps us explore our darker sides and fears as well as try on the antics of tricksters who gladly return to the briar patch or buffoons who get the golden goose. Ellen knows they help us learn our lessons as well. Just before the conference, she had returned from a summer in Israel where she was the youngest member of a contingent of students. I believe the story helped her as well as her listeners face some issues. G. K. Chesterton (1956) said of tales, "you will observe that one idea runs from one end of them to the other—the idea that peace and happiness can only exist on some condition. This idea, which is the core of ethics, is the core of the nursery tales." (p. 188).

Bringing Storytelling into High School

I wish they had never come to be called "nursery" tales, for folklorists who have traced that naming assure us that tales in ancient times were for all ages. When I introduce myths and folktales to adolescents, I try to show how the stories are ancestors of the literary works and songs and films we enjoy today. Attenborough's film *Cry Freedom* (1987) and Donald Woods' books, *Biko* (1978) and *Asking for Trouble* (1981), from which the film comes, might be explored as invitations into the ancient tales of Africa. From there students could move to American black folktales or to the trove of multicultural tales our libraries house.

When I invite high school or even middle school students into tales, I know only that I must bring an uncoated honesty—my own vulnerability—to our study. Then they, in turn, will bring theirs. Whether we are learning to tell myths and folktales, to recount events from our lives, or to try on the oral rhythms of poetry, I first tell samples myself. I also borrow library audio or videotapes or call on fellow teacher-storytellers to show the many styles of telling possible. I want to draw on what my students cherish from the days parents or teachers read or told or sang to them, but I want to push aside the negative "nursery" image of tales that some students bring as baggage.

I begin by presenting them a tale that is powerful for me and tell it as honestly as I can. Rather than *perform* it with a distance between them and me, I simply *tell* it—step inside it and invite them in. I rehearse the telling beforehand, and I do recommend that a teacher practice a story before telling it. But I try to avoid giving the impression that a telling is a product. Each telling differs from the next, and I want to model that storytelling is a matter of looking into the mind's eye for the images, sounds, and smells of the story and experiencing them anew. Then the story exposes who I am at that moment in time.

Because of the nature of perception, students will see me and the story through who *they* are, but I must choose the story primarily for myself. Teachers often ask me what tales "work" with older kids. Although I understand the pedagogical concern implicit in that question, I return again to the answer: The stories that touch *you* deeply will be the stories that touch your students. A list is not the answer.

What Does It Mean to "Learn" a Story?

For both teacher and student, learning a story means being able to walk through its key events from beginning to end. To accomplish that, we block out a story's plot, draw storyboards or maps using symbols and colors, and rehearse in mime. (Students form a circle facing out so they concentrate on themselves, not each other.) We often visualize our stories in silence with eyes closed. Then we divide into trusted pairs or threesomes for a first telling. I believe rehearsal must take place in class. I have had students continue to use storytelling as a mode of expression long after a unit is completed, just as Ellen did. They obviously rehearse at home. However, like writing, story-telling is a composing process. I want to be there to observe and question students as they compose, helping them work through to a trust of their stories. Some never do trust themselves or the story, exactly, but in the end even the shakiest of tellers breathes deeply and says, "I did it!" One boy wrote in his log, "I got sweaty, but no one laughed at me. I guess I did pretty good."

Teachers observe many levels of learning as they guide students through even one storytelling experience. (I recommend two consecutive rounds of telling because the second time through students improve markedly, building on the first telling's lessons.) Some students, it seems, complete the first telling mostly with a sense of survival. Just exposing themselves to the faces of their peers and living to tell about it constitutes a miracle. Later, they might wrestle with the hidden issues of greed and power, cruelty and foolishness which appear in the tales they choose. Some students will not admit they are facing issues about themselves. That's fine. It's the wrestling that is important. Some will indeed try on unfamiliar personalities in stories. One very serious, very "adult" 12-year-old, whom some students considered stuck-up, had the class guffawing when she told some of Richard Chase's *Jack Tales* (1943) as if she'd just come down from the hills in tattered overalls. Although she appeared to return at the unit's end to the quiet, self-possessed air she'd maintained before, I could tell no one, especially the boys, viewed her in quite the same light again. Something like the unnoticed girl who steps in as ringer on the boys' ballfield to the astonishment of coaches and kids alike.

Recording Layers of Learning

Learning logs, kept throughout a unit, in which students comment, question, notice, discover, and recount, add layers to the learning students do and teachers see. Below, some of Diane's (age 12) entries on the subjects of choosing and gaining confidence give a glimpse of how a student might approach thinking in such a log. I collect student logs on a rotating basis and write short comments when I do.

> I am having a little trouble developing the part where the boy's father finds out he has the death threatening disease that his Cherokee wife had before she died. The rest is pretty good. I just have to build up my confidence in my story.

I think I did pretty good on it except for one thing. The father is about to die, and he says (I said) in a choking voice, "I am going to die" which was pretty good until I blurted out, "I think." Everybody laughed.

Teacher response: Yes, our voices play tricks on us. Your story was very serious, Diane. Maybe subconsciously your mind said the kids needed a little comic relief. Concentration before an audience comes with practice.

The story that stood out most in my mind was Courtney's. Detailed, well said, with lots of hand motions.

I hope that when we tell the second round they won't be like the first ones. I am going to try telling a really jazzy story to brighten everything up.

I have read lots and lots of stories but the one book that stands out most is *Tales of Terror* by Ida Chittum (1975). It has 19 strange suspenseful terror stories. I might tell one of them, and they are good! I think the class will love them.

Mrs. S has read and we have watched lots of stories but I don't like the stories as much as the ones I pick. She reads such nice stories but I just can't picture myself telling one of them. But I am learning a lot.

Teacher response: Mostly, I'm trying to give the kids the idea of all the choices available so they will find a tale that really fits them, but it does take some looking independently. Sometimes I look for a long time before I find a tale I really love. Trust your instincts.

I am kind of stuck on this one story called "Print on the Window." It really is clever but it is very short.

I have changed a lot in the last few days. I am doing "Print on the Window." I learned that if you block things out you learn it better. I am much more confident in this story.

I am proud of my story and writing in this log has made me realize that I will be good in front of the class.

These are only some of Diane's entries. They focus mostly on her choosing. Other students write more about the rehearsal problems or successes they have, their reactions to specific exercises or readings they encounter in class. Some talk to me in the log. Others write to the log as they might to a diary (Schwartz, 1989). Many mention their anxiety about telling before peers.

What about Stage Fright?

I give my students a list of insights I've stumbled onto as I've worked through stories. The list includes five points to keep at hand when courage weakens.

1. Stories have taught me a lot about myself (Schwartz, 1985). Sometimes in the choosing I think I like a story, then something a character says or does or what happens in the end doesn't fit for me. That's a signal to drop the story or look more closely at exactly what is troubling. If I'm resisting part of the tale, it will be difficult to share honestly.

2. Trust your story. It will support you if you really care about it. Then trust the audience. If the story touched you in some important way and it continues to make you laugh or feel sad or brave or proud, it will have the same effect on the audience. Trust yourself. You will honor the story in your telling.

3. Think of your story as a gift, *not* a performance. When you give someone a gift you have specially chosen, you are excited because you are sure the recipient will value it. The spirit in which you give this gift will make the audience naturally appreciate it.

4. Experiment with the style of your story right up till the day of the large group telling. Tell it standing or seated on a stool. Tell it for your family, your dog, your bedroom's rock star posters or Degas ballerinas. Exaggerate your voice or gestures, then let them fall into a comfort zone where they feel natural but distinct. Think of the standup comedians or singers or speakers you have admired. They give their all. Give yours. At first you may feel self-conscious "hamming it up," but the audience yearns for the unusual. Make your telling something that is uniquely yours.

5. Have fun. Even if your story is very serious, keep reminding yourself to have fun.

Although the fact that each teller, including the teacher, is putting himself or herself on the line is probably enough to bring a community respect to the experience, I clearly invite the audience to:

1. Look into the eyes of the teller and respond naturally to the story. It's okay to enjoy the experience.

2. Remain seated during a telling so as not to break the teller's concentration.

Likewise, I invite the tellers to respect the audience by looking into their eyes and making room for their laughter or responses.

I understand the importance of feedback during and after a learning experience; however, I choose never to grade storytellings. We do much self-evaluation on our preparation and final tellings through directed log entries and short discussions. Students constantly watch each other and comment within the logs on what works and what interferes with a successful telling. Sometimes we critique videos of student or teacher tellers who have volunteered to be taped. However, giving grades during this unit adds a competitive element that I believe hampers cooperation and growth.

In *Clearing the Way*, Tom Romano (1987) points to the danger of just such a competitive spirit in a high school writing class:

> The discovery of our own possibilities helped everybody else discover theirs . . . But . . . If the sharing and pacing among students devolve into vicious competition, the creative atmosphere can turn stressful, crippling, and counterproductive. The pressure on students to compete with and beat each other will inhibit creativity. (p. 173)

Why Storytelling? Why High School?

I came to storytelling during my own high school years through extra-credit assignments during Shakespeare or poetry units. If you'd asked me or my teacher then if it was for everybody, we both would have said no. My teachers believed most teenagers hated getting up before their peers, and I would have hated to share the spotlight. (Not very many kids opted for the extra credit.)

Today I use storytelling with all my students. The ones who have difficulty composing on paper often shine in the oral or dramatic mode. Even the ones who've found comfort in the silent activities of reading and writing find release in the freedom storytelling offers. Each time they add a gesture or try an accent or hear their friends' approval for some stylistic nuance they have added to the story, they gain courage (Schwartz, 1987). Helping our adolescents value the sounds of their own voices and their ability to compose and revise their compositions, oral or written, we are helping them acquire the self-assurance they will need to live well in the world they soon face as adults.

Even more importantly, storytelling offers students the chance to know themselves by stepping into the world of literature. I will never forget what it felt like to try on the rhythms of Shakespeare without a book in my hands. Since high school I've told Japanese fairytales, excerpts from the life of Dr. Martin Luther King, parts of essays, and tales of my childhood. A classroom teacher can use storytelling as a way for students to taste the words of Alice Walker, Mark Twain, Leslie Marmon Silko, James Joyce, or Sylvia Plath. I love to invite students into the treasury of new, highly sophisticated picture books flooding the "children's" literature market, and, of course, I lure them to the dusty 398.2s where they find the stories dear to Appalachians, Tibetans, Mexicans, Eskimos, and South Africans. No matter where oral storytelling takes me and my students each year, we are marked indelibly by the rhythms and the deep meanings of the stories we encounter. Their images and messages sing in our bones and give us courage to face whatever trials or injustices the future may hold.

REFERENCES

Attenborough, R. (Producer-director). (1987). *Cry freedom* [Film]. New York: Universal Pictures.

Chase, R. (Ed.). (1943). *Jack tales*. New York: Houghton.

Chesterton, G. K. (1956). *All things considered*. New York: Sheed and Ward.

Chittum, I. (1975). *Tales of terror*. New York: Rand McNally.

Cohen, B. (1983). *Molly's pilgrim*. New York: Lothrop, Lee & Shepard.

Romano, T. (1987). *Clearing the way*. Portsmouth, NH: Heinemann.

Schwartz, M. (1985). Finding myself in my stories. *Language Arts, 62,* pp. 725–729.

Schwartz, M. (1987). Connecting to language through story. *Language Arts, 64,* pp. 603–610.

Schwartz, M. (1989). Storytelling—a way to look deeper. *English Journal, 78,* pp. 42–46.

Seeger, P., & Seeger, C. (1973). *The foolish frog*. New York: Macmillan.

Sendak, M. (1962). *Chicken soup with rice*. New York: Harper.

Woods, D. (1978). *Biko*. London: Paddington.

Woods, D. (1981). *Asking for trouble: The autobiography of a banned journalist*. New York: Atheneum.

Dispelling the Myth about Who Should Read Mythology

Joan N. Mittelstaedt

Menasha High School, Menasha, Wisconsin

Schools traditionally have reserved classical mythology and folklore for college-bound, advanced-placement, or "gifted and talented" students. Surveys by the National Assessment of Educational Progress indicate that 83.8 percent of students in the top quartile know about Greek and Roman mythology as compared to only 43.2 percent of students in the bottom quartile (Ravitch & Finn, 1987, p. 165). Some educators may interpret these percentages to support the "myth" that only college-bound students are able to handle the reading of classical mythology and folklore; however, in keeping with my own classroom experiences, these percentages reveal the reality that "low-track" students are not offered the study of classical mythology and folklore.

Lower-quartile students are more likely to be offered comic book and television heroes than classical heroes in low-track English classes. Without a doubt, these modern-day heroes have become a part of today's culture; however, I agree (and I believe my students would also agree) that Wonder Woman, Mr. T, and the Incredible Hulk "can't hold a candle to Odysseus, Medea, Achilles, Antigone, Oedipus, and Hector—or, for that matter, to any number of the historical figures who lived heroic lives and provide models of character and valor for young people" (Ravitch & Finn, p. 216). This article will illustrate how classical mythology and folklore can be experienced, enjoyed, and learned by high school students who have been tracked into low-level English classes.

Students prior to their junior year are tracked into "gifted and talented," average, or team (low) English in my school. Although some of my students had been in average classes for ninth- and tenth-grade English, most had been in "team English." Lack of school success (measured by grade points and class rank) is their common bond. Many low-track students, however, are above average in intelligence. Some are very bright and critically minded young people. Many have special talents for drawing and music and writing stories. Their lack of school success, for the most part, is a result of not handing in required work, not attending classes, and not conforming to established school tradition. Students are especially responsive to teachers who show an interest in them, who know they have ideas of value, and who allow them to express these ideas in meaningful ways.

The Art of Storytelling

Since myths explained occurrences in nature and taught traditions and lessons, storytelling is a natural way to approach mythology and folklore. Storytelling is a process that helps us understand our lives. Reading myths as stories to be told and then thought about, talked about, and written about (not merely consumed) becomes the very essence of the course (Meller, Hemming, & Leggett, 1984, p. 94). When students realize that they too can tell and write stories to explain events in nature and their own lives, their interest is often sparked. Inspired by *Changing Stories* (an excellent book that can be used to show how a story has different versions and meanings), I begin the semester with the following thoughts:

- This class is about myths, folktales, and stories.
- It is about who told the stories and who listened to them, and how the stories changed as they were retold by different tellers to different listeners.
- It is about what happened when the stories came to be written down and collected into books: about the writers and the collectors, and how the stories again changed as they were rewritten by different writers for different readers.

·   It is about what you have come to expect of stories, because you already know a lot about them—perhaps more than you realize.

·   When you were younger you enjoyed listening to and reading stories: Now, as well as reading for enjoyment, you are able to explore the meanings and messages of stories and understand how and why they have changed over the years.

·   This is important because stories are one of the ways by which we are taught about the world we live in and how we are expected to behave in it as girls and boys, men and women. (from Meller et al., 1984).

Through discussion of ideas like these, students build a framework for classical mythology as well as fairytales and their own personal stories. A close look at storytelling as an art helps students realize that our lives are shaped by the stories we tell and believe.

As a means to generate students' interest in stories, I use "hinting" or foreshadowing of story lines and heroes. I mention that many of the myths we'll read are about love as a source of conflict as well as pleasure. Briefly telling love stories involving Psyche, Penelope, Aeneas, or Zeus helps students anticipate future readings and arouses curiosity.

Students also enjoy writing their own stories using some of the classical myths as a basis. The following is an example of how to help students connect their lives with the stories they read:

> Having read Pandora's story and viewed the filmstrip about her, write an actual or imaginary incident involving yourself or someone else in a situation that brings out the symbolic meaning of Pandora. Some suggestions for a modern-day Pandora story follow:
>
> 1. a tragedy
> 2. a drug scene
> 3. a driving experience in winter
> 4. a day when everything goes wrong
> 5. a snowmobile experience
> 6. a day in school or an experience coming to school
> 7. a hunting accident
> 8. loss of a friend
>
> Note: Involve one or more of the evils that escaped Pandora's box in your story.

Following are a few stories woven out of "Pandora's Box" and students' lives:

When I was a little kid I used to go to the store which my parents forbid me to go. But I kept going and going even though I got punished every time, I did it. But I was so curious I kept going all the time even though they punished me every time. But finally I went one time knowing little did I know it would be my last time. I got caught and my step father beat me black and blue. From then on I never went to the store without my parents or my parents permission.

—Cory H.

A reverend had a son who had his liscense, but wanted a car. His son was a good kid so the reverend made a deal with him. He said, If you read the whole bible I'll get you a car. They agreed to the deal. A while later the boy said to his dad, I've finished reading it. But he never really read it. Then the dad said Oh you did? Then you should have the car. The son said why. The dad said cause in the middle of the book was a check stuffed in the middle of the bible for your car.

—Keith F.

My Pandora story is one of a dangerous curiosity. For four years my friend and I shared everything. We never deceived each other or talked behind each other's back. Up until our Sophmore year, things were great, our personalities complemented each other. But in the Spring of 1987 my friend got a new boyfriend.

Her new boyfriend not only pulled her away from her friends and family, but he got her very interested in drugs. When asked why she was doing this to herself she answered "I just wanted to see what it was like." Her curiosity grew to an addiction, a habit she couldn't break. She lost all her friends, her family turned against her, all she has left is her boyfriend and her cocaine.

—Jody P.

Questions (appropriate for beginning the semester) revolving around defining myths and their role in earlier civilizations help students think about Greek and Roman mythology:

- What is a myth?
- Is there any basis of fact in these myths, or are they pure fancy?
- Did the Greeks in the historical period accept without question the myths as they were handed down by tradition?
- Did the Romans play as large a part as the Greeks in the creation of these myths?

Comparing and contrasting the Greeks and Romans afford the opportunity to talk about how stories reflect the imagination of a culture.

This is also an appropriate time for students in large or small groups to describe the culture in which they live as reflected through television shows, advertising, and music.

Course Content

Ethnic backgrounds of students and the community are important to consider when selecting stories, especially in the areas of American folklore, ballads, and fairytales. Students may research tales and legends that they know from their own heritage. When students have an opportunity to actively participate in curriculum development, they begin to realize that they have ideas of value.

The following outline suggests course content and teaching sequence. This outline is not intended to limit curricular choices; it serves only as a possible list and grouping of stories. Many of the myths and tales are included in Edith Hamilton's *Mythology* (1952). In addition, various filmstrips, movies, slides, maps, and paintings supplement stories and are readily available through libraries as well as audiovisual and book companies.

Outline of Course Content

    I. Classical Mythology
        A. Introductory Material
            1. Classical Mythology: Questions
            2. Introduction to Classical Mythology
        B. Background of Classical Mythology
            1. Greek and Roman Deity and the Myths
            2. The Gods, the Creation, and the Earliest Heroes
        C. Stories of Love and Adventure
            1. "Cupid and Psyche"
            2. "Eight Brief Tales of Lovers"
            3. "The Quest of the Golden Fleece"
        D. The Royal House of Thebes
            1. "Cadmus and His Children"
            2. "Oedipus"
            3. "Antigone"
            4. "The Seven against Thebes"

II. Great Heroes before, during, and after the Trojan War
  A. The Great Heroes before the Trojan War
    1. "Perseus"
    2. "Theseus"
    3. "Hercules" (Drama: *Alcestis* by Sophocles)
    4. "Atalanta"
  B. "The Trojan War"
    1. "The Prologue"
    2. "Episodes of the War"
  C. "The Adventures of Aeneas"
    1. Introduction and Part I
    2. Parts II and III

III. *The Odyssey* by Homer (Fitzgerald translation)

IV. Norse Mythology
  A. "Introduction to Norse Mythology"
  B. "In a Northern Land"
  C. "The Great Gods"
  D. "The Norse Gods" and "The Creation"

V. Folktales and Ballads
  A. Folktales from around the World
  B. English and Scottish Ballads
  C. American Folk Ballads

VI. Fairy Tales and Fables
  A. Fairy Tales Today
  B. Fables: The Fables of Aesop

VII. American Folklore
  A. Modern Folk Heroes
  B. Indian Legends and Contemporary Folklore

Units I through V follow a natural progression of character and story-line development. "The Trojan War" introduces Odysseus and acquaints readers with his cleverness, which in turn prepares for his appearance again in the *Odyssey*. Units VI and VII, however, are interchangeable.

Making Connections through Expressive Arts

Approaching classical mythology and folklore through the storytelling process paves the way for other expressive arts (in addition to writing) such as drawing, drama, song, and sculpture. Projects and activities centered around these arts serve as a means for connecting learning with students' lives.

I require each student to submit one project related to our study of mythology. This project aids in understanding literary and cultural developments of the past as they relate to the present. Each student spends a minimum of three hours, exclusive of class time, on the research and construction of the project. Following is a list of suggested projects for students to consider:

1. Find five or more different poems in which the poet uses names or places of mythological origin. On 8 1/2 × 11 inch unlined paper, copy the title of the poem, the poet's name, and the portion of the poem (at least six lines) in which the mythological name or place is used. Under each excerpt from the poem, list the words from mythology and define them or give the mythological significance.

2. Find 10 pictures, labels, or news articles that contain the names of mythological gods, heroes, or places. Cut them out (Do not use library books!) and paste them, using glue or scotch tape, on 8 1/2 × 11 inch unlined paper. List the name of the Greek, Roman, or Norse god or character below the picture and state its position, mission, or significance.

3. Same procedure as No. 2 above, but use your personal talent to artistically draw mythological scenes, gods, or heroes.

4. Write 10 sentences using mythological expressions that are used in our language today (e.g., "Achilles heel" or "Herculean task"). Below each sentence, write the mythological connection or significance.

5. Find a musical composition, either classical or contemporary, that has mythological derivation or significance; and (a) write out and orally explain the mythological significance of the name, place, or thing; (b) arrange to play portions of it to the class (5–10 minutes). There are several classical recordings related to mythology in the library. Turn in your written explanation on 8 1/2 × 11 inch lined paper.

6. Complete a piece of art, sculpture, or woodcraft; original ideas are welcome, but clear them through the teacher.

7. Write a report on female characters in mythology and their importance and significance.

8. Another suggested project idea? Consult with the teacher.

Without a doubt, one of the highlights of the semester is sharing projects. Usually students display artwork and written projects in the school library and hall display cases. One semester, students did a special display of their work in the school board meeting room during National Education Week. The local newspaper took pictures of the projects with some of the students and wrote a feature story about them and their work. Another year, I videotaped students showing their projects and explaining the significance of their work to everyday life. Students displayed their projects at a local bank, and the videotape of students played throughout the day for the community to enjoy.

Another project idea revolves around holidays celebrated in the community. Working in small groups, students brainstorm holidays they celebrate and list traditions or customs associated with each holiday. Students select one tradition or custom and research it in order to discover the "story" behind it; in the process, students quickly find out that books are not their only sources of information. Interviewing grandparents and other adults is especially helpful. Each student is responsible for writing a brief report on the custom. Some of the students volunteer to type the reports; the class makes a booklet of holiday customs, and each student receives a copy. This project is fun to do, and it is an interesting learning experience for the students (and the teacher).

REFERENCES

Hamilton, E. (1952). *Mythology*. New York: The New American Library.

Homer. *Odyssey*. (1963). (R. Fitzgerald, Trans.). Garden City, NY: Doubleday.

Homer. *Odyssey*. (1963). (R. Fitzgerald, Trans.). Garden City, NY: Doubleday.

Homer. *Odyssey*. (1965). (K. Lynn & A. Jewett, Eds.; R. Fitzgerald, Trans.). Boston: Houghton Mifflin.

Meller, B., Hemming, J., & Leggett, J. (1984). *Changing stories*. London: ILEA English Centre.

Creating a Character: Performance-Based Oral Book Reports

Susan Gardner

Walla Walla College
College Place, Washington

We all want to be better teachers, to constantly improve and update our assignments and teaching techniques, but in the heat of a school year, it's hard to find time to reflect, reassess, and redesign. Being a teacher-researcher for my dissertation project provided the time necessary to step back and observe other teachers. Talking with them, I reevaluated myself. I gained valuable trade secrets that had a direct impact on my teaching.

Marcia Tomlin, one of my research subjects, was an experienced junior high school teacher. I often slipped into the back of her ninth-grade English classes to observe. One day, however, I attended an eighth-grade reading class. Eighth-graders can appear electrically charged at almost any time, but on this morning excited whispers, bulging sacks next to several students' desks, and nervous giggles pointed to some special happening. Marcia toned up with, "All right, class, we're ready to begin our book reports. You all know what you're supposed to do, right?" Two students slipped from the room; carrying their brown paper bags with them.

Was this an exceptionally bright group of motivated eighth-graders, or was I in some educational heaven where all students come prepared and ready to do book reports? There was no time to answer this question as I watched a blonde, bewigged 13-year-old slink back into the room, cigarette holder in her hand and newly applied beauty mark on her cheek. Her voice, lowered to a more sultry rasp, oozed, "Good morning. I'm Bette Davis, and I'd like to tell you about my life. After a few moments, you may ask me questions."

"Bette" gave a brief introduction of herself, including details from her childhood and a few highlights from her acting career. Her relaxed manner, her enjoyment of performing for yet another audience, was apparent as she lazily shifted on the high stool provided for her. Rarely glancing at prepared notecards, she gazed directly at the eager listeners, transporting them quickly to Hollywood and the big screen. When she opened the questions section, several hands raised immediately, and the game continued.

The game, it turned out, was the oral book report with a new twist. The class had been studying five books as a group—*The Diary of a Young Girl; Dandelion Wine; Bless the Beasts and Children; Farewell to Manzanar*; and *The Autobiography of Miss Jane Pittman*. All were in the biography-autobiography category, although the last is a fictionalized account of a person's life. In addition to the group study, each student selected a biography or autobiography to read outside of class and to share orally later.

The "later" was what I observed, and the success of this approach was astounding to me. I watched as well-prepared students and interested listeners reviewed and learned about significant parts of the lives of historical figures, athletes, musicians, and war heros. In a brief opening and with the lively give-and-take of questions from the audience, the life of Bette Davis unfolded to intrigued students and their teacher. No boring book reports here.

The obvious preparation and lively exchange between classmates were no accidents. I discovered that setting up for successful performance-based book reports took careful planning. Would this idea work with my semi-jaded sophomores as it had with Marcia's uninhibited eighth-graders? I couldn't wait to find out.

In the beginning, getting students interested in literature is often 90 percent investment of the teacher's personal enthusiasm and 10 percent an interesting dust cover. Once students are "into" a book, its spell takes over, but up to that point the teacher is usually the seller.

In her book *In the Middle*, Nancie Atwell describes wanting students to be involved in literature as a natural process of enjoyment, like "the dining room table" talk she and family members engage in over good books. How to project our enthusiasm for reading to our students, how to create "the dining room table," is the problem each of us faces as literature teachers. I, like Atwell, approached the business of introducing these book reports from a personal standpoint.

I love to read; I have always loved to read. I can't really remember a time when I couldn't read or a time when my world wasn't filled with books and stories and poetry. In fourth grade I especially remember devouring a set of orange-covered biographies on famous Americans. I have since discovered these books weren't always orange, but they all had black silhouette figures to show the characters and the action of the story. My first recollections of American history really came with these lives of Abigail Adams, Martha Custis and George Washington, Sacajawea, and Abraham Lincoln. My love of biographies was born from reading about these people.

I decided to capitalize on the interest most of us have for other people's lives. First, I boxed up a number of biographies or autobiographies I was currently reading at home, had read, or had purchased and was to planning to read. Second, I asked our librarian to fill a book cart with her latest and most-read biographies and autobiographies in a variety of lengths and reading levels. Students choose books not just by interest, or by fancy cover, but also by length. It's not just laziness. They are pragmatists; they know what they can accomplish in the period of time assigned for the activity. I wanted everything from big, thick books with small print to 125-page books with large print and an easier level of reading. In brief talks, the librarian highlighted a number of the books she brought, and I held up the others so that all could see the selections before they came closer to choose.

I allowed students to select books from home collections or the public library as well, as long as they were biographies or autobigraphies. I encouraged students to choose a new book, one they hadn't read before, and I didn't want any duplicates within a class because that would put students at a disadvantage when it came time for presentations.

I also told students that if they started a book, read a few chapters, and discovered it simply wasn't interesting, they could stop and choose another book. As much as I am a compulsive finisher of books, I recognize that I quietly set aside books that don't appeal to me with the intention that I will return to them later. Sometimes I do. Students should know how people really read—if they are to become lifelong

readers—and that includes discarding boring books. Rather than slog-
ging through a boring biography, I wanted them to become enamored
with their books so the oral presentations would be fun.

For the most part, my goals worked. When I gave students class
time to read, I didn't have to keep reminding them to "be quiet and
read." They were. Often when I would try to stop their reading to go
on with another class activity, they would beg for five more minutes.
The books had them hooked. Of course, no teacher expects success
with every student. There were still some reluctant readers and days
when a few students were "marching to the beat of a different drum-
mer." But that's to be expected with adolescents.

When it came time to introduce the book reports—about halfway
through their reading—they were ready for a new twist to an old
assignment.

"Let's try something different, class, for book reports this quarter,"
I began. "I know you've all done the standard type of report before.
You know, the two-page, neatly written blurb that begins with the
fresh, new opening 'My book report is on . . .' And you read it at sixty
miles an hour so that you can get finished and sit down while your
classmates and I are supposedly taking notes on birth and death dates,
numbers of children, accomplishments, etc." They nodded in agreement. It sounded about right to them.

"Not this time. Since you're all reading biographies/auto-
biographies, a perfect assignment would be to have you bring your
main character to life, really. In fact, that's what you're going to do. I
want you to become the main character of your book for your report.
You've been reading about what this person has accomplished in a
lifetime, but you should also have picked up on attitudes, opinions, or
feelings. You should be able to visualize the person physically. Most of
your books include pictures, and some of you are reading about
contemporary figures that you see on the news or in sports. What
about becoming that person for a day, well, really just part of a class
period?"

This did not sound like the standard book report to my wary
sophomores. The proposal piqued their natural interest as well as
suspicions, so I continued.

"Your presentation can be dramatized a bit. I know most of you are
hams, so use your natural acting talents. Wear clothing or bring props
that would suggest your character, and if you need help with this, I'll
be glad to provide it. I don't want you to spend a lot of money on
costumes. There's a good chance your family closets will provide

possibilities. Places like St. Vincent DePaul's and second-hand stores can also provide some unusual items at little expense.

"In addition, dressing up as your character isn't enough if all you do is get up and read your standard report to the class. They might have something interesting to look at, but the content would remain predictable. So, prepare to give about a minute intro to yourself—your name, who you are, when you lived and where. That kind of stuff. Then, the floor will be opened for questions from the audience so that the details of your life will be fleshed out and we will really know you as a person."

A ripple of excitement mixed with anxiety raced through the classroom. This idea didn't sound quite as easy as the stock report format. It even meant that students would have to read the whole book. They couldn't choose what parts they would highlight in a very brief, prepared two pages. They would be open to all sorts of questions from their peers. It's much easier to fool a teacher in a book report assignment, but classmates? Definitely a new twist.

The idea of dramatizing the character seemed to meet with a good deal of enthusiasm. Almost immediately there was a buzz among the students about what they might wear to portray their characters, questions about borrowing such and so from members who had X, and excitement about make-up, hair, and props. Anxieties surfaced in two areas: What kinds of questions would be asked, and how would the presenters be graded?

If these two concerns aren't taken care of, they can ruin the enthusiasm and the presentations. We created a list of appropriate questions that could be expanded on as the character up front suggested. We practiced the questions a bit, and what presenters should do if they didn't know the answers because the information wasn't in the book they read. Students are rather clever in their replies when they have read their books carefully and have truly become involved with their characters. One day, a not-very-alert student asked a character what had caused her death, and she came back with a sardonic grin and replied, "I don't know. I haven't died yet." The class' good laugh caused the questioner to wake up to what was going on.

Our list of questions grew from the stock ones of "How many children did you have?" and "Who were you married to?" to "What would you rate as your most significant accomplishment in life?" Students wanted to know such things as "How would you want to be remembered in history?" or "If you could live one moment in your life over again, what would that be and why?" Although some of the answers might seem to be speculation on the part of students, often their books would reveal high points or moments of discouragement that they could easily select and explain from the point of view, actual words, or feelings of the character as described.

Having the audience ask questions served many purposes. Most obvious, of course, is that the audience participated instead of dozing in their private corners. Then, too, it kept the presenters on their toes. They couldn't go to sleep on their own reports, and they didn't dare not read their books. They had to face their peers, and no sophomore wants to be embarrassed by peers. They knew they could answer, "I don't know. It wasn't in my book," once in a while to questions, but that couldn't happen too often.

Teachers often worry about the agonies shyer students go through in up-front projects. Amazingly, however, when shyer students assume roles of other characters, they are often much less inhibited. If asked to get up front and present themselves, they nearly collapse, but being someone outside themselves seems less threatening, and they often do a remarkable job.

Another plus to getting audience participation is involving quieter class members. I awarded points (1/2 point per question) to questioners, and I selected three or four main questioners for each speaker. These people were to lead the way, and then, after the major questions were asked, others could join in. That way I passed the questioning responsibility around, and vocal people didn't dominate every presentation or rack up all the questioning points.

The element of dramatization helped the book reports become performance. Actors are affected by the feedback they receive from their audience, and knowing that classmates were truly interested and listening helped students become animated in their presentations. The use of costumes, props, and body language stimulated ingenuity in class members who wanted to do as well as other presenters.

I would be dishonest if I didn't admit to some failures. There were one or two students who didn't bother with costuming of any kind, and one fellow ran desperately to the P.E. department to borrow a tennis racket between classes so he could be Jimmy Connors. To his classmates, he was no Jimmy Connors. His knowledge of the tennis pro's life after his cursory presentation was a decided flop, but he was the only flop in 29 book reports in his class.

Grading is another area of concern. It provides some motivation, but it can paralyze some shyer students. I tried to alleviate anxiety by providing the criteria presenters would be graded on, broken down by possible points for each section. Several days before the presentations were to begin, I distributed a grading sheet and spent much of one class period describing my expectations carefully. On it I asked them to fill in their names, book titles, main characters they would be portraying (often titles don't provide clues to this), and the due date of the presentation. I wanted to reinforce the latter as often as possible so students wouldn't make mistakes on when to be ready. After going over the main sections of organization and clarity, preparation, interest, visual aids, and delivery, I collected the grading sheets and then arranged them in order of presentation.

I needed to create for myself one additional chart so I could keep track of questioners' points. To help me be very organized once the presentations started, I put asterisks by questioners for each speaker and told the students whom they would be questioning ahead of time. Each day I reviewed the characters to be covered the following day to remind both questioners and presenters of their responsibilities and to provide some publicity for the "coming attractions."

Her black pillbox with a touch of netting to cover her eyes, her hair smoothed into an almost chignon, her ruby red lips, black taffeta tailored evening suit, and her black gloved hands told me Cynthia was no more. She gazed calmly but determinedly at her audience and announced, "My name is Wallis Warfield Simpson. I am a divorced American woman who made quite a stir in Great Britain in 1936, for, you see, I am also known as 'the woman he loved' so much that he gave up his crown for me. Who was he? Edward VIII, of course, King of England. Now what else would you like to know about me?"

I settled back at my uncomfortable student desk and began to write comments on Cynthia's grading sheet. Recording who was asking questions brought a quiet smile to my face. "Mrs. Simpson" and audience were thoroughly involved in her life story. What could be more interesting than an enthusiastic student's presentation? For the moment, nothing.

A Noncritical Thinking Approach

Patricia P. Kelly

Virginia Tech
Blacksburg, Virginia

"Well," Jayne offered timidly, "I think Richard Cory is like a bus stop bench."

"Yeah," Jon said, "a bus stop bench is all dressed up with signs and all, not like a park bench. The poem says that Richard Cory glittered when he walked."

Angie continued, "A bus stop bench is always a busy place with people coming and going, but the bench stays there; it's not really a part of it all, you know. That's how Richard Cory felt. He didn't feel a part of the things around him or connected to people."

With those observations, my class launched into the "pretending game" we play as a way to noncritically analyze literature. The pretending game is a class activity where the students and I try hard to believe an improbable assertion, inference, or comparison and to help find ways to support rather than refute it.

Noncritical analysis, of course, is a paradoxical notion. When we analyze, we examine critically, detect, prove, refute, and most of all disbelieve until we have an assertion that stands up to all measures of doubt. Ironically, such critical analysis is a stance quite different from Coleridge's notion that readers must willingly suspend their disbelief, or doubting, to experience literature.

My noncritical approach has its genesis in a classroom and a teacher in my memory. I can still smell the oiled wooden floors and see in my mind's eye the flicker of a smile lift the corners of her mouth as she settled back and let the discussion go after provoking a heated debate.

On this particular occasion the class was discussing *Vanity Fair*, and I was arguing vehemently that Becky Sharp was a "survivor," using whatever it took to manage in a world she never created. The young men in the class hooted derisively at my notions, and we argued hotly and loudly.

Some years later I modeled my own teaching style after hers but with one difference, a difference that changes the process of thinking critically. I wanted a classroom like hers where students responded to students' assertions, not to the teacher's questions, where students felt passionate about ideas and risked taking stands and seeing things differently. But I also wanted a class where students listened and pondered the ideas others presented, rather than merely waiting for their opportunity to refute what had been offered. I remembered my frustration in that long-ago schoolroom when it seemed that all the boys in the class were against my idea. No one listened to the points I made; all were framing their arguments and waiting for the opportunity to interject them; everyone was bent on proving me wrong instead of at least acknowledging the "truths" lurking at the edge. So for my students I began the pretending game, which includes a noncritical, believing, pretending process that for a few moments halts debate and refutation and makes students ponder instead possibilities or even impossibilities.

Noncritical analysis is imbedded in other familiar strategies, for example, brainstorming. Brainstorming requires participants to withhold critical commentary on suggestions because we know that good ideas are cut short by a rush to judgment. It seems to me, however, that even in that process we skip a step when we go directly from the creative, imaginative stage of brainstorming to a critical analysis of the ideas generated. Students engaging in the creative process know that shortly those diverse ideas will be tested, examined, and evaluated. They may decide, consciously or unconsciously, to offer safe, defendable suggestions instead of risking an outlying view they feel unprepared to defend. The pretending game, therefore, becomes an intermediate step. Following the brainstorming, we look at the ideas on the board and select those that are different, or as the students say, "off the wall." We then pretend we believe those ideas, considering each separately and offering reasons for its validity.

With each new class, one of the first things I teach is how to play the pretending, "believing" game. This fall I walked into class, pointed to the concrete block wall, and announced that the wall was, in fact, a mural painted by an artist inspired by Mondrian. I asked the students to try very hard to "see" the wall as an artistic rendition. Students talked about what they saw that made the wall artistic and listened as others talked, trying hard to "see" the same things. Once someone noticed that each block had two unfilled grooves, which made a pronounced vertical and symmetrical black pattern, others became visibly excited about the game. The ivory paint became a mono-chromatic design evoking a feeling of "cool warmth," they offered, delighted with their oxymoron. They enthusiastically thought of ideas that dealt with form, function, and aesthetics. That wall, of course, finally remained an unattractive institutional artifact, but for a few moments it had become something different, and I don't think they can ever see it exactly as they did before the game. The mental exercise allowed us to see something we hadn't seen before; it allowed us to break down a fixed view of what was.

Following the activity, we talked about critical thinking, a process based on doubting, questioning, and seeking proof, and the difference in the kind of noncritical thinking they were doing in the pretending game. They agreed that if they had immediately offered logical reasons against the idea of the wall as a mural or otherwise proved the wall to be just a wall, we would have missed seeing the wall as we did. They also agreed that learning to play the game with something, in this case the wall, that held no conviction for them was easier than if they had had to set aside fervently held beliefs to engage in the activity.

Once students feel comfortable with it, the game becomes an integral part of our literature study. It is particularly effective with helping students learn how to evaluate the inferences they make. Ironically, this noncritical thinking approach might help students more than a critical thinking approach, perhaps because it is nonadversarial. The confrontal stance embedded in critical thinking sometimes frustrates, even angers, students, and they often resort to statements such as "Well, you just don't agree with my opinion [idea, conclusion, inference]" or "I have a right to my opinion, and it's as good as anyone else's." With noncritical thinking, when we put all the ideas on the board and try hard to believe in and support each one, students see which inferences are better, more logical, more accurate. The better inferences are easier to believe and support, but because the approach is nonconfrontal students don't feel threatened or intimidated by the process.

For example, in the discussion on "Richard Cory" above, one student compared Richard Cory to a teaspoon. We started trying to believe that metaphorical inference. Students played around with the idea that Cory probably would have felt more comfortable living life in small doses (i.e., teaspoons). Even though students tried to offer points of support, it soon became evident to the metaphor's proposer that the comparison was not based on a reasonable inference.

Generally the metaphors come from an activity I use called "more like." I create five or so paired comparisons, and students select one in each pair and generate reasons supporting each choice based on the literary text. Then they identify the one comparison for which they can build the best textual case. For example, for Richard Cory I had given them the following:

Is Richard Cory more like a park bench or a bus stop bench?
more like autumn or winter?
more like a teaspoon or a fork?
more like a closet or a hallway?
more like a cookie or cake?

We discuss the textual support for both comparisons in all the pairs. Then from the students' selections of the best ones, we begin "believing" each one and generating as much supportive material as possible by making inferences that can be even remotely tied to the text. With this teaching strategy, Richard Cory, or any character, takes on a life larger than that on the page, but all the inferences are reasonably drawn. Students are engaging in analogic thinking, making well-supported inferences, using their imaginations, and learning the complexities of characterization embedded in a few images and events.

A noncritical thinking approach is equally effective in discussing literature selections that evoke contrary inferences about events. In a recent discussion of John Updike's "A&P," for instance, I asked students why they thought Sammy had quit his job. One group of students held to the idea that Sammy's action was based on principle: He was making a statement about discrimination and standing up for those discriminated against. Another large group of students believed that Sammy was just showing off for the girls, trying to get their attention and making them indebted to him for his heroic action. We played the pretending game with each of the inferences. In this case, students offered good textual reasons for each inference. But in the process they were listening to each other instead of waiting for their chance to refute what was just said. They decided these two inferences were the best from those considered, and they learned to accept the ambiguity of having no single right answer or even answers, just good suppositions. On the way out of the room that day, one student said, "This class is like jello." I laughed at the aptness of the metaphor. For someone who needed answers, our class discussions were indeed slippery, with ideas no doubt squirting away just as he thought we had them pinned down.

The point of this process, however, is to suspend disbelief long enough to consider other ideas, ideas that may later be rejected but at least will have received thoughtful consideration. There are times when we debate, refute, argue, and confront interpretations and ideas. But other times we sit and listen and try very hard for a few minutes to believe the improbable. For like Alice in *Through the Looking Glass*, our students have difficulty believing unlikely contraries. "I dare say you haven't had much practice," said the Queen. "When I was your age I always did it for half an hour a day. Why, sometimes I've believed as many as six impossible things before breakfast. . . ."

FAMILY MATTERS

Susan Beth Pfeffer

In a world where so many of us differ on so many different things, one thing we all have in common is family. Everyone has one. You start out with one,—some combination of parents, siblings, grandparents, aunts, uncles, cousins, and pets. We all have different mixes, and the kids being born today have variations none of us ever dreamed possible, but basically we all have families. Later on, of course, many of us marry, and then we have additional families to deal with, as well as creating new family members. No wonder things are so complicated.

I doubt this is news to any of you, since you come here with your own family histories firmly in place. And if by some chance some of you are space aliens, and this is your first time on earth, you could learn a great deal about family structures just by watching an episode or two of *Dallas*. The only reason I bring it up is because I write books for children; and for children, family is the most important structure in their lives. So families abound in the books I write about.

What I'd like to do now is divide up family units into their individual parts—mother, father, brother, sister, and so forth, and discuss how these people fit into my books. I must warn you, I'll be lapsing into autobiography almost constantly, but don't panic. There will be no overhead slide projections of my parents' golden anniversary party.

Let's start with mothers. Mothers are pretty basic things in a family. I have 31 published novels, and in 30 of them, my main character has a mother. None of these mothers is particularly like my mother. There are a lot of reasons for that, starting with the fact that my mother used to type all my manuscripts, and I would have felt awkward if she noticed I was stealing a few of her more interesting character traits and turning them into fiction.

But there are other reasons as well. My mother is the best mother of grownups I have ever known, and she and I have been extremely close ever since that golden day when I left home for college and we no longer had to share a house. Up until then though it had been armed warfare. My most deeply held wish when I was 12 was to be an orphan. Now I grant you my experience with orphanhood came from *Anne of Green Gables* and Shirley Temple movies, and the orphans in those situations always ended up pretty happy. Some rich aunt takes them in, and after a period of adjustment, hearts melt, dolls are purchased, and happiness reigns. There isn't a single scene in *Pollyanna*, for example, where Pollyanna and her rich aunt are sitting around watching TV and Pollyanna's aunt drives her crazy by offering a running commentary on what's happening on the screen. "See, she told Perry Mason she went into the store to buy some nailpolish, but actually it was poison." Pollyanna simply never had to put up with that. Mothers were put on earth to drive their adolescent daughters crazy. Aunts who took in orphaned nieces were put on earth to thaw out and learn to love and then generally spoil said orphans until they and the readers ran out of tears. They said things like, "Oh Pollyanna, Rebecca of Sunnybrook Farm, Anne of Green Gables, my life was empty and meaningless until you moved in, and now every day is filled with joy and I could never hope to repay you for all you've given me, but with every breath of my being, I'll try. What do you want first?" In my wildest fantasies, I couldn't imagine my mother saying that.

Neither my mother nor my father was willing to give in to my needs and die when I wanted them to (by the way, I was an equal opportunity orphan, and would have cheerfully sent my older brother off with them), and they are all still very much among the living. Which is all for the best. But it limits my mother's usefulness as a character in my books.

The mothers in my middle-group books are essentially level-headed, loving women. Janie's mother in *Kid Power* is having a problem or two, but they come from unemployment and clearly will pass once she gets a job. She does make a lot of tuna noodle casserole, which is my personal idea of culinary hell, but she really likes Janie, and that shows throughout the book. I'm not convinced my mother much liked me when I was that age, and to be perfectly honest, she had no cause to like me. I was pretty repulsive back then.

Another difference between my mother and the mothers in my books is that my fictional mothers don't kill the food they're cooking. My mother is a great typist, but a vegetable to her is something that comes frozen in a box and needs to be cooked for half an hour to 45 minutes until any shade of its natural color has vanished into memory.

Broccoli, string beans, carrots—they were all brown. And meat should not so much be broiled or roasted as made to look as if it had just starred in *The Towering Inferno*. I occasionally take surveys of people my age, to see if their mothers knew how to cook, and the impression I get is that my mother was the rule rather than the exception. Maybe it had something to do with World War II.

But in children's books, mothers always know how to cook, meals are balanced, and there is almost never any mention of how good a typist the mother is. Nowadays these mothers frequently are brilliant nuclear physicists, or dynamic politicians, but they all steam their veggies, and none of them types. Then again, even as a kid, I never thought my parents might be normal.

Fathers. My father is a pip. I use him all the time, tiny, censored versions of him. But whereas when I was a little kid I might have been able to delude myself that my mother bore some relation to the mothers I knew best—June Cleaver, Margaret Anderson—my father was about as much the average television father as Mister Ed.

For starters, my father has always been bald. Even in his high school graduation picture you can see the shadow of future baldness lurking about. My mother has a passing resemblence to Harriet Nelson. At best, my father looks like Uncle Tonoose.

Then there's the matter of clothes. On television, when Jim Anderson came home from the office, or Ward Cleaver, he'd keep his tie and jacket and shoes on. Ozzie Nelson never went to work, so he didn't have to wear a tie, but all those other TV daddies dressed for success even while putting out the garbage.

My father is an internationally recognized constitutional lawyer. He's argued many cases before the Surpreme Court, has testified in cases in England and Australia, has written books that are recognized as the standard texts in their fields. He'd come home from the office, kick off his shoes, pull off his tie, peel off his jacket and shirt, and then step out of his pants. When he was wearing nothing but his undershirt, shorts, and socks, it was time for dinner.

Now the fathers in my books keep their clothes on, and they aren't bald either. But a hefty percentage of them are lawyers. They are also very proud of their children, as my father was of me, except when I was failing my classes or not keeping my room clean. The father who is most like my father is Janie's in *Kid Power*. Her father is furious with her when she goes around the neighborhood telling everyone how poor her family now is. He worries about her when she takes on odd jobs, and then he brags to one and all when she proves to be a success.

That's just how my father would have acted under similar circumstances. Only he would have done it with fewer clothes on.

The other thing about fathers in my books is that they are, if not distant, then at least not clinging. Father might know best in my books, but he doesn't go around telling people about it. Again, this reflects my childhood. It isn't that my father kept quiet those words of wisdom that fathers are supposed to hand down to their daughters. It's more that the lessons he passes on to me are limited in their applicability. "Tuition credits are unconstitutional" is a good one, or my personal favorite: "If the first word in an acrostic puzzle is three letters, then the odds are the word is 'the.'" Not exactly Polonius' farewell speech.

So the fathers in my books tell their daughters to be brave or honest or to respect their commitments, but they do it with the mothers present. Maybe I'll work on that in an upcoming book.

Siblings. Siblings are my favorites. Siblings come in four varieties— older, younger, brother, sister. I specialize in older. Sometimes the siblings I write about are brothers, sometimes they're sisters. But they're always older and they're almost always vicious.

I took a little survey of my books and here are a few of the things my older sibling characters say to my heroines (saints, each and every one):

"I know one favor you can do for me. You can drop dead."

"You have a real big mouth and a real small brain. That's a dangerous combination."

"Are you crazy?" he asked. Then he shook his head sadly. "Stupid question. Of course you are."

"First of all, you have to be sixteen or under," he said. "So you certainly qualify for that. If they were doing it on mental age, you'd qualify for six or under even."

And finally, in its classic simplicity:

I walked to Carol's room and knocked on her door.

"Go away," she said.

Remember my big brother Alan? I certainly haven't forgotten him. He's been the source of inspiration to me in my writing. I hand him the straight lines—his insults pop right back at me.

My classic childhood memory is of Alan twisting my arm until I'm screaming in pain, and my mother saying, "Susan, stop bothering your brother." Such was childhood for me.

In none of my middle-group books do my main characters have a younger sibling. I certainly know younger siblings exist, but I ignore them for a variety of reasons. First of all, although I was a perfection of a child, my memory of my friends with younger brothers is that my friends spent a lot of time saying things to their brothers not dissimilar to what my brother said to me. And I'd rather not show my heroines in such an unpleasant, if realistic, light. They're more appealing as victims.

Then there's the age problem. My main characters in my middle-group books tend to be 11 or 12 years old, so if they had younger siblings, those characters would be 9 or younger. And frankly, I don't understand little kids. The littler they are, the less I understand them. Two-year-olds will have lengthy conversations with me where I figure I'm lucky if I catch one word in five, and I'm sure I lose out on a lot of their more-subtle nuances. Kids a bit older than that talk better, but they don't have a great grasp of facts. I spent a week in Wyoming once, and since they don't get many writers visiting there, I was recruited to speak to every child in the school district. I explained to the kindergarteners that my picture book, *Awful Evelina*, was about cousins and asked them if they had cousins. One little boy raised his hand and said he did. How many? I asked. Ninety-two, he replied. Now I don't know much about Wyoming family structure, so I asked how many aunts and uncles he had. One, he said.

Frankly, I didn't believe that kid then—or now. Winters are long and boring in Wyoming, but that's 18 years of quintuplets and one off-year of twins, and I have my doubts. I can only assume that the kid made it up, and I don't know why anyone would make up a story like that. Which only goes to prove I don't understand six-year-olds.

Then there are nine-year-olds. (I grant you this is skipping ahead a little, but take my word for it, I don't understand seven- or eight-year-olds either.) I have two sets of friends, one with a nine-year-old boy, the other with a nine-year-old girl. Danny's conversations with me are always about transformers. "See, you take his head off and put it under his knee and he becomes a space shuttle. Then you take his left arm like this and you turn his head around and now he's a 20 megaton atomic bomb." Jenny's conversations are much more level-headed. "I won't wear that red dress! I hate it. Mom always makes me wear ugly clothes. Mom has the worst taste ever. I hate Mom!" We can all hardly wait to see what she's like when she's a teenager.

Probably the reason I don't understand younger kids and avoid so writing about them is I don't much remember myself at those innocent ages. Sure, I have memories of me before sixth grade, but my general impression of myself is pretty hazy. I guess I started becoming interesting to myself when puberty hit. Before then, I certainly wrote stories, but I wasn't my own best heroine. By sixth grade, I started watching as well as participating. All writers watch at least as much as they act. We are all living notebooks, filled with potentially useful observations. I observed family, friends, teachers, and myself. And largely because I had no choice in the matter, I observed my brother.

The older siblings in my books are all my brother. Now I don't want you to think Alan was a heartless monster devoted to making my life an eternal misery. He certainly was a heartless monster, but he had lots of interests other than torturing me. He played the flute and touch football, read Spinoza and got straight As, and in his spare time twisted my arm.

All younger siblings know life is inherently unfair, which, when you're writing from the viewpoint of a kid, is a great thing to be aware of. Life is unfair to children, because children are powerless. Until they get control of their bodies, they fall down stairs and trip over their own feet. They have to go to school whether they want to or not, and study things whether the subjects interest them or not. If their parents move, they move. If their parents divorce, then they lose at least part of one parent. They're served brown vegetables and leather-tough meat. I have seen children burst into tears of frustration because they've been taken to Chinese restaurants that don't serve chow mein. I've seen children weep with terror because their mother's car was stuck in the mud. Childhood really is awful.

But for younger siblings, not only are you perpetually losing to your parents on the major issues of life such as bedtimes and required baths, but in addition, there's this other kid in the house who gets to stay up later, beats you at games, knows more than you even dream of learning, and gets a bigger allowance than you all because he's older.

I met a writer once who told a class of eighth-graders that writing is revenge. I have no idea if the eighth-graders knew what she was talking about, but I understood instantly. Writing *is* revenge. I write about the cruelty of older siblings, and with every word I get a little harmless revenge.

There may be some people out there, older siblings or kindhearted humanitarians, who are worried about how Alan takes this treatment. For the most part, pretty well. He's not real thrilled when I get interviewed by the local paper in some place like Wyoming and the reporter writes down a few of my choicer anecdotes about what he did to me, but then again, I never show him those articles. I show them to my parents, and they show the articles to him. So I'm hardly to blame.

On the other hand, I actually felt a pang or two of guilt about how I was portraying Alan, so in my book *About David*, I put in a truly wonderful older brother, someone very much like Alan at his best—caring, sympathetic, supportive, an older brother a sister can count on. Alan read the book, then asked me if he was the basis for that character. I assured him he was.

"That's not me," he said, sounding slightly disgusted.

There's no pleasing older brothers.

You may notice that in my books when an older brother or sister is really needed in an emergency, he or she always comes through. The warfare is mostly verbal. That's just the way it is with family.

Grandparents. My characters have very few grandparents, and what few are mentioned hardly ever show up. Janie has a grandmother in *Kid Power*, but I don't know what becomes of her in *Kid Power Strikes Back*. (Frankly, I had forgotten about her by the time I wrote the sequel.) When grandparents are mentioned in my books, they're mostly people to whom newspaper articles extolling the virtues of my heroines will be sent. (In *Kid Power*, Dad says he's going to pick up a half-dozen copies of the paper to send to grandparents. I guess he forgot Janie had a grandmother in town too.)

What few other grandparents I've written about all seem to live in Florida, presumably so I won't have to deal with them. There's a lovely set of grandparents in my novel *The Year without Michael*, the grandmother constantly battling with her daughter-in-law; and in a new novel of mine called *Turning Thirteen*, there's a happier pair of retired grandparents. What these two sets of grandparents have in common, in addition to Florida condos, is answering machines. I seem to have decided that if I must write about grandparents, they shouldn't have to answer the phone. It wasn't until my most recent book, *Rewind to Yesterday*, that I had a grandparent who was alive and well and a major character. After 31 books, I suppose it's about time.

The reason for lack of grandparents in my stories is a lack of grandparents in my life. My father's parents were both dead by the time I was born, as was my mother's mother. That left me with one grandfather, and he too was not what I had been brought up to expect a grandparent to be like.

We all remember Dick and Jane. Dick and Jane and Spot too had legendary American grandparents. They lived close enough to be visited at Thanksgiving, and Grandma baked and Gramps whittled or drove a one-horse open sleigh. Gramps also fished when he wasn't whittling. Grandma presumably cleaned the fish when she wasn't baking her pies and cakes and cookies. She wore an apron, he wore overalls. They never once complained about their daughter-in-law and how she was raising the kids. They both had white hair and not only did they look their age, they looked 20 years older than their age. They were true American grandparents.

My one and only grandparent had a thick gray beard, and a thicker gray accent. He was born in Russia, and I'm sure it was a Russian accent, but my mother, who certainly knew him better than I did, claimed it was a Southern accent, since he lived in Winston-Salem, North Carolina. Whatever it was, he was unintelligible to me.

My grandfather, who had had a brief successful career as a junk dealer before retiring, was born in a Russian village midway between Minsk and Pinsk. I was born in New York City. We didn't have a lot in common, even if I could have understood what he was saying. I saw him once or twice a year, never at Thanksgiving, and never once did he whittle. Frankly, he scared me, and possibly I scared him. But mostly he disappointed me. He wasn't a Gramps. It was bad enough not having a Grandma to call my own, but my father's oldest sister looked real old to me and baked, so she served as a surrogate. But my one true grandparent never stumbled out of the pages of Dick and Jane.

When I grew up, I moved into a house where my next-door neighbors were true Gramps and Grandma. He wore a railroad cap; she baked; and I adored them. I suppose if I were looking for traditional grandparent figures to put into a book, I could use them, although it might be more fun to use the one grandparent I ever had. There have got to be kids out there with inappropriate grandparents. I can't be the only one with a midway-between-Minsk-and-Pinsk forebear.

Aunts and Uncles. What I lack in grandparents, I more than make up for in aunts and uncles. Boy, do I have aunts and uncles. Twenty-two of them in fact. I dedicated *Courage, Dana* to the entire lot of them, and nary a one thanked me. I love them anyway.

My family specializes in aunts. My mother has three sisters and a brother; my father has seven sisters and a brother. One of my father's sisters, and my mother's brother, never married. The rest did, which is why the total adds up to 22.

My mother's sisters are all very pleasant quiet people, so there's no point talking about them. My father's sisters, on the other hand, are the stuff legends are made of.

For starters, they all looked the same to me when I was a kid. You have to understand how it is with kids and how it is with families. You're expected to know everyone, but nobody ever introduces you. Now if you have just one aunt and uncle you can probably figure them out pretty easily. But if you have seven identical aunts, whom you see a couple times a year at family screaming orgies and nobody ever says to you, "The one screaming in the corner is your aunt Dot, and the one screaming in the kitchen is your aunt Rose," then it's hard to figure out just which one is which. To make matters worse, my uncle Hy and my uncle Mac looked like identical twins and they weren't even related. It took about 12 years before I figured out Hy was the one who pinched, and that was how you told them apart. I still can't tell Rose apart from Dot.

Pfeffers love to scream. For the most part, they very sensibly choose mates who don't love to scream, and therefore don't offer them much competition that way. Pfeffers will scream about anything. They scream about how wonderful their children are. They scream about politics. They scream about the weather, about books, about whatever's around to be screamed about. Each and every one of them knows he or she had the single worst childhood. They especially love to scream about that.

As it happens, Pfeffer is the dominant gene. That's what happens when you choose quiet mates to reproduce with. So we cousins are all screamers too. Of course, what Pfeffer children scream about mostly is our parents. And they provide us with endless material.

Given the vivid quality of my aunts and even a few of my uncles, it's amazing how few aunts and uncles pop up in my books. In *Just between Us*, there's a Great Aunt Doris who is quite clearly based on Anna and Shari and Lil and Rose and Ettie and Millie and Dot. But she just makes a special guest star appearance and is never heard from again. To some who don't know better, she's hardly more than a plot device.

The obvious reason for this lack of aunts and uncles is generational differences. She isn't even Aunt Doris; she's Great Aunt Doris. I'm older than the characters I write about. In a few ghastly years, I'll even be older than my characters' parents. In any event, the aunts and uncles of my characters are people of my generation, and no matter how hard we try, we'll never be quite as lively as my father's sisters.

Cousins. With 22 aunts and uncles, you're thinking, she must have lots of cousins. I have a fair amount, but perhaps not as many as you might think. Twenty-three in all. Those 22 aunts and uncles, all coming as they did from large families, chose not to reproduce with the fervor of their parents. Of course, many of my cousins have spouses, a couple even have former spouses, and they've reproduced too. So with cousins, cousins by marriage, former cousins by marriage, first cousins once removed, and babies of first cousins once removed, the numbers add up.

I love having cousins, and I'm quite close to a couple of them in particular. Cousins have many of the advantages of siblings, shared family histories and childhoods, with few of the disadvantages (although my cousin Fran has complained of being jealous of my brother too, since he was held up to her as perfection incarnate).

Cousins don't exactly litter the pages of my books either, although I keep meaning to put some in. The scene with Great Aunt Doris has Cousin Andrea in it. Cousin Andrea, age 16, is a very realistic character. Cass, the book's heroine, reports that for the past five years, whenever her family has gone over to visit Andrea's, Andrea has always been in her bedroom studying for a test. Even in the summer. I had several dozen cousins just like that. It was a stage most Pfeffer cousins went through, me included. Practically the only time I voluntarily studied was when the alternative was visiting my father's family.

One of my books is actually based on my experiences with my cousins, and that's my picture book *Awful Evelina*. I wrote *Evelina* when I thought picture books must be easy to write because they were so short. That was before I realized that I have no understanding of the little kids who make up the characters in picture books. *Awful Evelina* is based on my two first cousins once removed, David and Alan. I feel I should point out right now that all my male cousins are named David, Alan, Arthur, or Richard. That's it. When I wrote *About David*, my mother went crazy. She pointed out to me that I had three cousins and one uncle named David, and it was hardly a tribute to them to write a book where a boy named David kills his parents and himself. "Can't you call the book *About Donald*?" she asked, but of course the answer was no.

Anyway, this particular pair of David and Alans are never called David and Alan because they have the misfortune to be the only pair of twins in the family. They're the sons of my cousin Eileen, and as best I can figure it out, they must be in their early thirties. One of them, David I think, is married and a father. But they weren't always grownup. It's a little hard for me to believe they're grownups now, because I didn't lay eyes on them for 15 years while they were in their rooms studying for a test. It's a family tradition.

The twins were pudgy little kids, and vicious too. I guess it must be hard being the only set of twins in a family, especially if you have the exact same names as everybody else, so you get called The Twins simply to differentiate yourself from all those other Davids and Alans. Before the twins were old enough to hide in their rooms studying, they had an adorable habit when forced to greet their older first cousins once removed. David would get on one of my feet (or Fran's, or my brother's), and Alan would get on the other, and they'd grind down. Such actions were clearly deliberate, almost ritualistic. There was always a lot of screaming going on whenever the family got together, so no one heard our shrieks of pain (or if we were heard, we were ignored). Because the twins were considerably younger than we were, and because their twin status guaranteed that they were thought of as being cute, it never occurred to any of us to complain about the damage being done to our toes. I do feel I should point out, though, that not a single Pfeffer cousin ever became a ballet dancer.

In *Awful Evelina*, David and Alan become Evelina, the dreaded cousin. Fiction's very handy that way. I turned two boys eight years younger than I into one girl cousin my main character's age, but I gave to Evelina all of the twins' least appealing habits. Of course by story's end, Evelina and Meredith are close friends, whereas the best I can say about the twins is whichever one it was who got married had the best single wedding I've ever been to.

Let me tell another cousin story that while it's never made it to any of my books has a certain literary quality to it. One of my 23 cousins is Ellen Conford. She's the daughter of my father's older sister Lil, so she's as much a Pfeffer as I am.

When I was a kid, Ellen was a big cousin to me. A big cousin was anyone older than my brother. People older than Alan were unapproachable in my eyes, the age difference was so vast. Ellen hung out a lot with my cousin Fran's older sister Judy, another big cousin, and at one major family occasion, probably when some Richard or Arthur got married, Ellen and Judy ate orchids. They must have been around 14, and one or another of them had read about orchid eating in some romantic 1920s novel. After they ate the orchids, it occurred to them they might die from orchid poisoning, but I'm delighted to report that they both survived. However, this burst of romantic derring-do made a big impression on both Fran and me.

Many years pass and Ellen ceases to be a big cousin and becomes just a cousin instead. Our careers have a certain amount of overlap, and on occasion we find ourselves at the same professional party. A couple of years back, we were at a party at the New York City Public

Library. There was a high school reporter there, grabbing interviews with the various children's book writers in attendance. She spoke to me for a couple minutes, and then I brought her over to meet Ellen.

"This is Ellen Conford," I said with perfect little-cousin mischievousness. "When she was a teenager, she ate orchids."

The reporter didn't leave Ellen's side for the rest of the party.

I have one other classic cousin story involving Ellen and me and Judy's daughter Mindy. Mindy was 11 or 12 and she went to her local library to see if they had the newest Judy Blume. Alas, it was already out.

"Have you read any books by Ellen Conford?" the librarian asked Mindy. "I'm sure you'd like her."

"Ellen Conford is my cousin," Mindy replied. "So I've read everything by her."

"Well isn't that interesting," the librarian said. "How about Susan Beth Pfeffer? Have you read anything by her?"

"I've read everything by her too," Mindy said. "She's my cousin also."

"Well in that case, you certainly don't need any help from me," the librarian huffed, and walked off to recommend books to some kid without delusions of famous relatives.

Pets. Anyone with pets knows pets are definitely part of the family. I have two cats now, and cats do pop up in my books. I got my first cat when I was in college. His name was Dashiell Chandler Lardner Agee Fitzgerald Cat Pfeffer (I had literary pretentions), and he was a deeply neurotic cat. As a kitten, he spent the first six months of his life hiding under my bed. He'd come out to eat and that was about it. But since he was my first cat, I could only assume that all cats were like that, and when I wrote my first book, *Just Morgan*, and put a cat in it, I described Dashiell to perfection, little suspecting that Dashiell was the feline who put cat into catatonic.

Years after Dashiell's death, my friend Christy, who had known Dashiell from kittenhood (a relationship based mostly on lying on the floor, peeking under the bedspread, and being stared at by a pair of terrified kitten eyes), mentioned to me that Dashiell was far and away the most neurotic and disturbed cat it had never been her pleasure to know. And she had liked Dashiell.

"Why didn't you tell me?" I asked her. Like all good mothers, I automatically assumed my pet's problems were the direct result of my own inadequancies.

"I never had the heart to," she replied.

I wouldn't mind so much if Dashiell hadn't been immortalized. What if some poor kid out there who'd always yearned for a cat read *Just Morgan* and learned that kittens spend their early years hiding? Who knows how many Humane Society kittens have met an early end because of my literary efforts? It's clearly all Christy's fault.

Every now and again a dog makes a quick appearance in one of my books. I certainly like dogs, but since I've never lived with one, I don't write about them. For quite a while, I realized, none of my characters had pets. I kept forgetting to put them in. So lately I've been throwing in cats. I had a recent tragic experience with tropical fish, so at some point I'll throw a fish tank into a story as well.

As a kid, I had no pets. My father was officially scared of dogs and cats, and my mother made it clear she felt it was concession enough that she had had children and saw no reason to deal with animals also. Of course I yearned for pets, especially a dog. Everyone from Dick and Jane on had a dog, and if I was going to be cheated on grandparents, the least my parents could do for me was give me a puppy.

Naturally my parents didn't see it that way, and until I was 12, the only pets we were allowed were salamanders and toads. The toads ate the salamanders, and then we'd take the toads back to civilization, and they'd die too, so my mother was very happy.

By junior high, I was deemed responsible enough to handle animals, and soon I had parakeets, guppies, and hamsters. My mother took over the guppies when I found I couldn't deal with their habit of eating their newborn (in retrospect, I find it a bit chilling that my mother grew so fond of them), but the birds and the rodents were mine, and I took reasonably good care of them.

My father took occasional business trips, and he came home from one of them, when I was in high school, with a smile on his face. He was bursting with a secret, and without too much effort on my part, he told me the surprise. While in Florida, he had purchased a pet alligator for me.

Now this is a man who claims to be scared of kittens. He is married to a woman who has sworn never to have a house pet larger than a shoebox in her house. He's father to a boy who announced his freshman year in college that if a dog entered the house in his absence, he wouldn't come home for vacations ever. This man buys an alligator. I can only assume male menopause was responsible.

To give my mother her due, she didn't immediately sue for divorce. The alligator was being shipped, so we had some time to find out all we could about our friend the reptile. We went to the local pet store and bought How to Tend for Your Alligator booklets. The basic rules seemed to be keep it in your bathtub, don't flush it down the toilet, and when it gets big enough to chew your hand off, donate it to the neighborhood zoo.

Sounded fine to me. Granted an alligator wasn't likely to be cuddly or to bark in ecstasy when I got home from school, but it was certainly lively and distinctive. So I looked forward to the arrival of my newest pet.

A couple weeks passed, and finally the alligator arrived in a plain brown wrapper. I opened the box, and found one dead alligator waiting for me. We buried it without ceremony in the backyard, and my father never bought me another pet again.

What especially fascinates me about this is what would have happened if my father hadn't told me an alligator was coming. He wanted it to be a surprise, after all. Can you imagine what I would have felt if, without any warning, I opened a box addressed to me, with no return address on it, and found an alligator, living or dead, in it? I wasn't that secure an adolescent anyway. A girl could take something like that personally.

That pretty much covers the whole family spectrum—mothers, fathers, siblings, grandparents, aunts, uncles, cousins, and alligators. It's been a little disconcerting for me to realize that I who have such vivid relatives have barely written about any of them in my books. On the other hand, it's reassuring to know that if I ever need material, all I have to do is remember some dreaded incident from my childhood, and I'll have enough for a family saga or two. That is, if I can beat my cousin Ellen to the material. Not to mention my father's long-threatened autobiography.

Oh dear. I'd better get to work right now. Catch me later, and I'll be happy to show you volume two of The Sound and the Pfeffers.

Notes on Contributors

Arthur N. Applebee is a professor in the School of Education, State University of New York at Albany, and Director of the Center for the Learning and Teaching of Literature. He specializes in research on language use and language learning, particularly as these occur in school settings.

Gill Clarkson, after 45 years in schools (as pupil, teacher, coordinator, and now trainer for the Knowledge About Language element in England's new English National Curriculum) is enthusiastic about all who want to learn and the many ways they do so. Her current struggles with an M.Phil. dissertation remind her constantly that the learning process is hard and that learners need all the help we can give.

Bill Corcoran holds that it doesn't make a lot of sense to keep composition and literature apart, as if they didn't swim in the same sea of English. At least that's the way it looks from "down under" where he works as Senior Lecturer in English Education at James Cook University, Townsville, which is only a couple hours away from the Great Barrier Reef. There the fish and the coral seem to know they depend on one another, and the ocean that supports them both, for survival.

Susan Gardner has taught for a decade and a half, from junior high to university—primarily English, speech, and drama. Currently she teaches English and coordinates writing at Walla Walla College. Combining her love of literature and writing is her interest in children's books, written primarily for her expressive young son, Montgomery.

Patricia Kelly, a middle school and high school English teacher for more years than she cares to admit, currently teaches English education courses at Virginia Tech. She is Director of the Southwest Virginia Writing Project, and her publications range across the English language arts spectrum. An inveterate gardener, her goal is to replicate Dora's fields in her own Wordsworthian space.

Judy Lightfoot works diligently to maintain her status as a perennial amateur in the profession. She teaches English at Lakeside School in Seattle, and she's taught secondary and college students for 20 years. Her mystification about how people learn deepens over time but is leavened by two persisting insights: that she teaches writing better when she herself is writing, and that she teaches even familiar literature better while trying to read works from cultures and authors foreign to her experience.

Gretchen Portwood Mathews has taught English, journalism, and reading to students in grades 8 through 12 for the past 15 years in Fairfax County, Virginia. She's currently involved in a teacher-researcher program sponsored by the Northern Virginia Writing Project. She is curious about how pop culture influences reading and writing, and about the difference between what her kids call "real reading and writing" and "doing an English assignment."

Peter Medway taught English in secondary schools for many years, but always with one foot in some other camp such as social studies or humanities. Hence his interest in trying to produce accounts of English that are intelligible to people in other disciplines. Since giving up real work he has been at Leeds University, writing, researching, and coordinating a project. His other foot is now in technical and vocational education, and especially design and technology education.

Bruce Miller, a colleague of Jim Collins at the University at Buffalo, spends much of his professional life studying the connections of art, language, and reason and much of his private life enjoying the companionship of his cats, Junkets and Dolly.

Joan Mittelstaedt has taught for 17 years and speaks professionally on behalf of so-called low-track students. She is a doctoral student at New York University and recently lived two summers in England with her son, gathering experiences for storytelling.

Charles Moran has been teaching writing and literature since 1958—in secondary school, in graduate school, and at the University of Massachusetts at Amherst. He has directed programs and chaired departments, but finds teaching the essential activity. Among his recent achievements: a decision to end his term as director of the university's Writing Program, and a refusal to join AARP.

Susan Ohanian played alto sax in a college dance band, dropped all interest in sports when the Dodgers left Brooklyn, and does not know Roman numerals past XXIX. She has never met a cat she doesn't like or a reading incentive she does.

Susan Beth Pfeffer wrote her first book, *Just Morgan*, her last semester at New York University. Since then, she has written over thirty books for children and young adults. Among her titles are *Kid Power, About David*, and *The Year Without Michael*. As further indication of her interest in family, she has recently completed work on *The Sebastian Sisters* Quintet.

Tom Reigstad's dad sold office furniture and stationery supplies, and Tom formed a strong bond with paper, pencils, and desks. In 16 years of teaching, he's tried to share his enthusiasm for writing and its paraphernalia. He's in the English Department at Buffalo State College.

Marni Schwartz is a storyteller because she is a rememberer. She was taught to write at a very young age by a grandmother whose joy was writing letters, taught to step into her fantasies by a father whose joy was springboard diving, and taught to trust in the likes of three billygoat brothers by a mother whose joy was gathering children around a flannel board. She has worked since 1973 with middle schoolers and traveled widely as a storyteller. Her greatest joy is watching learners delight in their rememberings.

Andrew Stibbs has taught in Britain for more than 25 years. The first half of his career was spent teaching English to teenagers in schools, and the second half has been spent educating teachers at the University of Leeds. He has published on teaching English, especially literature, and on children's literature and poetry.

Ruth Vinz is currently working on a collection of short fiction. Ruth believes that teachers who try to write literature teach differently from teachers who do not. She's learned through practice that it's impossible to prescribe what students should write. "There is something vaguely dishonest in school writing. I learned that when I started writing myself."